LEADING
POSITIVE
CLASSROOMS

DR CHRISTOPHER HUDSON

LEADING POSITIVE CLASSROOMS

Adopting an educative approach to behaviour management in schools

© Christopher Hudson 2024

All rights reserved. No part of this book may be reproduced or transmitted in any form or by any means, electronic or mechanical, including photocopying, recording or by any information storage and retrieval system, without prior permission in writing from the publisher.

Published by Amba Press
Melbourne, Australia
www.ambapress.com.au

Editor – Brooke Lyons
Cover Designer – Tess McCabe

ISBN: 9781923116375 (pbk)
ISBN: 9781923116382 (ebk)

A catalogue record for this book is available from the National Library of Australia.

PRAISE

'Christopher provides a comprehensive, well-grounded research basis for how we lead for behaviour and learning in the classroom. He pursues the practical realities of behaviour leadership from a sound psychological and humanitarian basis. A particular strength of this book is that it grounds the crucial theoretical with the essential practical. I commend this book for both beginning teachers and those well into their teaching journey. Those who teach undergraduate teachers will also find this book a most valuable resource in equipping future teachers who take on the crucial professional role of teacher-leaders in schools.' - **Dr Bill Rogers, Behaviour Specialist and Education Consultant**

'This book calls for a rebalancing of the power dynamics in classrooms, seeking first to understand a child's behaviour before proactively supporting them to thrive. Christopher takes a holistic approach to behaviour education and, in doing so, he challenges the longstanding notion of the authoritarian teacher. He argues the need for teachers to build positive connections with students to provide a pathway for them to flourish as learners.' - **Lauren Davis, Deputy Principal, St John's Primary School**

'Christopher adopts a student-centric approach, highlighting the significance of nurturing relationships, fostering teamwork and building collaboration to adeptly meet the diverse needs of today's learners. The text melds whole-school behaviour strategies with practical, classroom-ready methodologies. Whether you are about to embark on your teaching journey or have traversed many years in the profession, this book is the ideal companion.' - **Dr Tom Porta, Lecturer in Initial and Continuing Teacher Education, Flinders University**

'Having learnt from Christopher as a leader in student management roles over the years, I can attest to the power of the strategies and tips that he lays out in this book. This is a must-read for all educators.' - **Jarrod Warmington, Teacher, Brunswick Secondary College**

'Christopher demonstrates the importance of building relationships with all stakeholders, teaching classroom routines and transitions, and acknowledging students' positive contributions in the classroom. A must-have for beginning teachers, experienced teachers and school leaders to build a whole-school behaviour education approach!' - **Natalie Baker, Learning and Teaching Coach, Christ the King Primary School**

'Christopher has provided a path into behaviour education that is progressive and positive rather than punitive. It is heartening to see a framework for building a culture of connectedness that can help students flourish. This is a must-read.' - **Jacob Storer, Teacher and Year 12 Leader, Leeton High School**

'If you've read any of Christopher's work, you'll know that he has a way of making research relatable and easy to understand. This book is no different! It is full of examples and practical frameworks. Most importantly, for me as a principal, it honours the importance of leaders and teachers working together to build relationships with students and their support networks.' - **Timothy Mulhall, Principal, Marlborough Primary School**

'Through reading this book you'll become more confident in your ability to adopt a behaviour education approach in your classroom. A highly recommended read that gives insight into how to positively impact the lives of students and to ensure deeper connections in the classroom.' - **Steven Mclaughlin, Teacher, Rosebud Secondary College**

ABOUT THE AUTHOR

Dr Christopher Hudson is an experienced educator, school leader and researcher who is passionate about transforming education through evidenced-based practices and professional learning. His journey into education has not been linear; he worked across multiple sectors and in different roles prior to entering education.

From 2005 to 2007 he completed a carpentry apprenticeship and worked as a site manager for a large commercial construction company in Melbourne. In 2009, he commenced work as a Constable for Victoria Police, which is where he developed a passion for working with disadvantaged and marginalised young people. He studied a Physical Education degree at Victoria University from 2011 to 2013 and then completed a Master of Teaching (Secondary) at Federation University in 2015. In 2021, he completed a Master of Education (Leadership and Management) at the University of Melbourne. Christopher's doctoral research, also conducted at the University of Melbourne, was focused on investigating successful school leadership in rural Victoria, Australia.

As a school leader, Christopher specialised in creating and facilitating community-based personal development programs for young people who were at risk of disengaging from school. His ability to form strong school-community relationships resulted in many young people broadening their skill sets, developing positive relationships in the community, (re)engaging with mainstream education and building positive conflict resolution skills.

In 2023, Christopher received the ACEL New Voice in Educational Leadership Research Scholarship, which recognises emerging leaders in the field. He has published academic papers and book chapters in several areas of education: the intersection of sport pedagogy and social justice, professional learning communities, teachers' use of data to inform practice, and rural school leadership.

Christopher is currently working as a lecturer at Federation University, teaching units across the Master of Teaching and Bachelor of Secondary Education (Health and Physical Education) degrees. Through his lecturing and consultancy work, he aims to empower both teachers and students to maximise their potential for high-quality teaching and learning in schools.

ACKNOWLEDGEMENTS

At the time of writing this book I was simultaneously writing a doctoral thesis, working and raising two very energetic young boys under three. When I reflect back on this stage in my life, I realise that there is no way I could have done all of that without the beautiful friends, family and colleagues I have around me. Lots of people took some of the load off me so I was afforded the time and space I needed to write.

First, I would like to acknowledge my partner, Lauren. Thank you for the support and love that you have shown me during the busiest period of our lives. You often had to take on a lot so that I could focus on what I needed to do to write this book, and I am deeply grateful for that. I hope this book has much impact in the field and makes all that time worth it. I also hope that our boys are proud of what we have achieved together.

Second, I would like to thank my parents, Susan and Matthew, and step-parents, Brett and Danielle. You all sacrificed a lot so that I could have an education, which was often at the expense of your own education. You have given me more opportunity than I could have hoped for in life and for that, I thank you immensely. This gratitude also extends to my parents-in-law, Maria and Michael, for their support, love and encouragement during both the doctorate and this book. Thank you.

Third, I would like to thank Alicia Cohen from Amba Press for taking a punt on me when I said I had an idea for a book. Your support, guidance and leadership throughout the whole writing process was second to none and I am thankful to have worked with such an energetic, professional and knowledgeable person. You got the very best out of this wordy fella.

Last, to my two children, Billy and Harvey. I want to reiterate how much I love you and how incredibly proud I am to be your dad. You fill my life up with so much joy and I want to thank you for making me the luckiest person on earth. I love you both immensely and everything I do is for you.

Without you all I would not be in the position that I am now.

Thank you and much love to you all.

CONTENTS

Preface	A letter of hope	**xiii**
Introduction	A case for change	**1**

PART I: Everything is relationship   13

Chapter 1	Building referent power through high-growth relationships	**17**
Chapter 2	Engaging in the mesosystem	**45**
Chapter 3	Becoming a trauma-informed practitioner	**71**

PART II: Walking the wire   93

Chapter 4	Preventative practice strategies	**97**
Chapter 5	Correction strategies	**127**
Chapter 6	Restorative practices	**163**
Conclusion	Statement of action	**179**
References		**185**

PREFACE

A LETTER OF HOPE

Dear teacher,

I write this letter to you as a message of hope. I hope that you find value in what I have written and enact the strategies herein. I hope that you read these pages and feel confident in your practice as an educator to work in any school, be that primary, secondary, rural, urban, low SES, high SES, Catholic, government or independent. Wherever you land, my hope is that you find this book supportive – like a mentoring voice in your ear to let you know that the profession values you and your impact on students.

One of the reasons I wrote this book is that, when I first started out as a teacher, I received absolutely no behaviour education training. It was, essentially, a case of 'Don't smile before Easter and you'll be right.' I'm not joking. That advice was given to me on several occasions. I like smiling, and I like to do it a lot before Easter, so I am telling you to not listen to this ghastly guidance! Smile large and smile often. Teaching is a wonderful profession, and you have the ability to make an impact on the lives of the young people who cross your path.

The other reason I wrote this book is that, when I began writing it, my partner and I were in the process of choosing a school for our son, Billy. While going on school tours and thinking about what I would hope for in a school, and, indeed, in a teacher for him, three things came to mind: respect, kindness and unconditional positive regard.

In the end, I knew that I would want a school and its teachers to adopt an approach to behaviour management that was educative rather than punitive. There will be many times during their schooling when our two boys will look to others for love, support and guidance, and my hope is that they are treated in a way that supports them to achieve whatever it is they want to in life. One of these people might be you, as their teacher.

This book has also been an opportunity for me to think back on my time as a Constable for Victoria Police and, importantly, as an educator. One thing that I have learnt across both roles is that human connection is by far the most powerful force in this world. There truly is no substitute for treating each other with love, dignity, respect and kindness. I have approached being an educator, especially in student management roles, in much the same way as if I were a mentor or coach. I have seen my role as someone who is there to guide students when they need me the most, shining a light on some pretty dim paths sometimes. I have experienced great success in doing so, and much of my approach is documented in this book.

It is my genuine hope that this book inspires you to adopt an educative approach to behaviour management as part of your practice.

Dr Christopher Hudson

INTRODUCTION

A CASE FOR CHANGE

'I can't change the direction of the wind, but I can adjust my sails to always reach my destination.' – James Dean

Behaviour management is an essential skill for teachers. Student misbehaviour in the classroom is progressively interfering with teaching and learning. Over the last decade, student misbehaviour has been a core driver of teacher attrition (Paramita et al., 2020). It is concerning, especially given the current educational climate in which some schools are unable to fully staff themselves.

In April 2023, the Organisation for Economic Co-operation and Development (OECD) released its *Education Policy Outlook in Australia* report. While Australia's school system is generally considered to be high-performing in relation to other OECD countries, one of the most salient findings in this report was that Australia's classrooms are among the least favourable in terms of disciplinary climate, measured by students' perceptions of how often noise and disorder occur in the classroom. The report refers to data generated from the OECD's 2018 *Teaching and Learning International Survey* (TALIS), explaining that 37 per cent of secondary school principals in Australia reported that intimidation or bullying among students occurred at least weekly. The report also stated that Australian teachers feel less prepared than their peers across OECD countries to manage disruptive classroom behaviour.

Our declining disciplinary climate in Australian schools is coupled with high teacher attrition and declining student academic performance. The report considered evidence from a Commonwealth issues paper on teacher shortages (DESEM, 2022) and claimed that by 2025, Australia will have a 'projected deficit of 4100 secondary school teachers'. The report paints a grim outlook for the state of education in Australia – student disengagement and misbehaviour are on the rise, which is contributing to high teacher turnover, and the associated supply challenges are putting an increased strain on the entire system.

A key recommendation from the OECD report was the urgent need to support teacher development in classroom management to drive improvement in the culture of Australian classrooms. If we are to change the culture of our schools and lead positive classrooms, we must seek to improve things for the betterment of ourselves as educators and our students as learners. Paramita et al. (2020) argued that although the importance of behaviour management skills is covered in most pre-service teacher education programs, it is generally considered to be too limited or lacking practical value. Others (Baker, 2005; Egeberg et al., 2016) have emphasised that experienced teachers need to engage in ongoing behaviour management professional learning for the implementation of classroom management practices to have a positive effect on students' misbehaviour.

This is our collective case for change, and it is where this book makes its contribution. It serves as an entry point for beginner teachers, and a practical resource for more experienced teachers, too.

The movement towards behaviour education

You will notice that in this book I have chosen to shift focus from the term 'behaviour management' and instead use the term 'behaviour education'. There is a good reason for this.

While I recognise that student misbehaviour is disruptive and difficult for both teachers and students, I firmly believe that we must flip our lens on how we view it. Yes, there are times when we must 'manage' student misbehaviour, but, for the most part, there is plenty we can do to educate students before any form of management is needed. If we are seeking to manage behaviour as a first port of call then we are missing the opportunity to provide students with valuable opportunities to learn how to self-regulate. Most importantly, our times have changed and we must adapt and evolve how we approach student misbehaviour.

Behaviour management in schools has largely mirrored societal expectations of human behaviour in other arenas of life – particularly the world of work. As we progressed through the industrial revolution, there was a need to 'produce' docile bodies who were capable of working in factories, and the management of these bodies matched the disciplinarian regime at school. Extrinsic motivation ruled. There were strict hierarchical regimes – where a top-down approach governed subordinates, rewarding 'good' behaviour with pay and punishing 'bad' behaviour with fewer hours or, worse, no work at all. Schools enacted much the same processes, rewarding 'good' behaviour and punishing 'bad' behaviour through segregation, detention and a loss of privileges. Thankfully, the crude authoritarian approach of corporal punishment was abandoned in the 1980s as cultural and social norms shifted; however, so much of what we do in schools has not kept pace.

Managing bodies in and through school like an assembly line is no longer appropriate given the current epoch we are in. However, progress in schools has seemingly moved at iceberg pace over the last hundred years and, shamefully, much of the factory model of education still haunts us today. I shake my head every time I walk past a classroom with rowed seating, I question the role of uniforms and I wonder why we continue to segregate students into age-based groups. I believe that teaching students through individual, siloed subjects is outdated, and I wonder if there is a better way to structure the school day away from the factory-like set-up where we need a bell to remind us of a 15-minute morning recess and a 45-minute lunch break.

Perhaps these are broader issues that need to be explored in another book, but you get where I am going with this. We must be critical of ourselves as educators and of the system that governs us. It is, largely, an education system that is no longer fit for purpose. We know this and yet we still continue to do what we have always done because we know no other way. How can we expect different results if we don't critique what it is we are doing and change our approach? This is the definition of insanity.

In his text, *Ideology and Curriculum*, Michael Apple (2004) urged us as educators to continually critique our practice, particularly considering schools are interconnected with other institutions – political and economic – that dominate our society. He said:

> Since schools often unquestioningly act to distribute knowledge and values through both the overt and hidden curriculum ... it is a necessity for educators to engage in searching analyses of the ways in which they allow values and commitments to unconsciously work through them.

Over the years, there has been some shift towards a more developed understanding of attending to student misbehaviour in schools, stressing the importance of positive relationships and ensuring that the school culture is responsive to students' emotional needs. However, the focus still tends to be largely on enforcing behavioural compliance through exclusionary disciplinary practices (e.g. detentions, suspensions and expulsions) and a conventional rule-based system rather than adopting an educative approach, especially in Australian classrooms (Lewis et al., 2005). While certain rules in schools are needed because they help us to lead positive classrooms, as well as ensuring that both teachers and students stay safe and engage positively together, Raby (2012) emphasised that some rules are tired and serve little purpose in modern-day society (e.g. excessive regulation of dress), and some can also reflect and perpetuate inequalities and students' beliefs about young people.

This reliance on punitive measures is justified on the basis of 'deterrence theory' (see Pratt et al., 2006; Raskolnikov, 2021), which posits that the threat of punishment can discourage and divert students from engaging in certain behaviours. However, exclusionary disciplinary practices often fail to consider the complexity of factors that contribute to a student's behaviour, such as socioeconomic conditions and the delicate interplay of family dynamics (Raby, 2010, 2012). We also know that this approach contributes to negative learning and wellbeing outcomes for students (Gregory et al., 2010a; Skiba et al., 2014; Talwar & Lee, 2011), especially for students from marginalised minority and ethnic groups (Gregory et al., 2017; Nicholson-Crotty et al., 2009; Skiba et al., 2002) and for students with disabilities (Krezmien et al., 2006; Skiba et al., 2014).

In their review of the literature on the effects of exclusionary disciplinary practices in schools, Skiba et al. (2014) found that use of these practices was a risk factor for negative developmental outcomes for students. Alarmingly, this included an increased risk of repeated involvement with the juvenile justice system (the 'school to prison pipeline'). The authors found substantial empirical support for four themes related to exclusionary disciplinary practices in schools:

1. Exclusionary disciplinary practices are widely used and are increasing in frequency, especially for day-to-day disruptions such as ongoing defiance and non-compliance.
2. There is consistent evidence of disproportionate exclusionary disciplinary practices experienced by students with disabilities and students from minority racial and ethnic groups.
3. The use of exclusionary disciplinary practices is a substantial risk factor for further negative outcomes, such as academic disengagement and lower academic achievement, which may cascade over time.
4. Exclusionary disciplinary practices are in and of themselves a developmental risk factor, above and beyond any behavioural or demographic risk factors students bring with them to the classroom. Thus, research suggests that there exists a level of intentionality, tacitly or overtly, behind the consequences associated with exclusionary disciplinary practices – in other words, they further marginalise the already marginalised.

With regards to the last point, we see that exclusionary disciplinary practices act as a 'technology of power' (Foucault, 1977) that (re) produce the dominant societal power structures in and through the *'dispositif'* (Foucault, 1977, 1980) of the education system, which includes both discursive and nondiscursive elements and the relationships between them over time.

Exclusionary disciplinary practices have been found to be more commonly associated with the behaviour of adolescent male students (Gregory et al., 2010a; Krezmien et al., 2006; Skiba et al., 2002). In their longitudinal study of over 4000 student referrals leading to exclusionary disciplinary practices in one school district in the United States, Skiba et al. (2002) noted that female students were significantly more likely than male students to be referred to a school leader's office for only one of the possible infractions requiring exclusionary disciplinary action – truancy. The study showed that male students were more likely to be disciplined for a wider range of infractions, ranging in seriousness from minor but ongoing classroom disruption through to fighting, vandalism, sexual acts, indecent exposure, threatening or obscene language directed toward others, and throwing objects. While many of these behaviours are very concerning and most definitely warrant in-depth investigation and follow up, using exclusionary disciplinary practices as a means to deal with them does not result in positive developmental outcomes, and is not associated with a reduction in subsequent misbehaviour (Gregory et al., 2010a; Skiba et al., 2002). Indeed, a punitive environment has been found to be associated with students seeking only to lie and conceal further transgressions (Talwar & Lee, 2011). Additionally, does it not seem paradoxical to exclude a child from school who might have low school attendances in the first place? Exclusionary disciplinary practices are odd practices to adopt and their place in schools needs to be critically challenged.

If we know that this approach doesn't work, why is 'popular punitivism' (Campbell, 2015; Martin, 2010) still in existence in schools? Well, to some extent the liberalisation of behaviour management has been no match for the growth of a rigid, high-stakes testing culture that dominates much the education landscape, especially in Australia. The pressure of test-based accountability systems in this country (e.g. NAPLAN and ATAR) sees students pushed along a pipeline of schooling until the sum of their efforts culminates in a single numerical score at the end of 13 years. In some ways we can argue that we have evolved with behaviour management (e.g. we place more focus on student wellbeing) but in other ways we have in fact hardened our approach in and through our highly pressurised education system. Behaviour management has become synonymous with getting students to do what we want them to do – sit down, focus intently, engage with the content (regardless of what it is – *this is the knowledge you need to know*), and produce good academic results. We reward that as the norm and we seemingly punish deviance from it, whether that be overtly or tacitly.

However, reports such as the one previously mentioned from the OECD (2023) demonstrate that this approach is not working for us in Australia. Returning to 'normality' post COVID-19 has seen higher levels of student disengagement. Many teachers are burnt out, and there is a growing disconnect between what the system wants (or, some might say, what it 'forces' upon us) and what students and teachers value in education. In this environment, a reliance on exclusionary disciplinary practices will serve no good.

We must change, and we must change now. As part of this change I stress that we need to see behaviour as a skill that needs to be taught, modelled and practised. Teaching students about positive behaviours needs to occur alongside the core skills of literacy and numeracy – it is no different. The goal of schooling is not just to prepare students to be capable of contributing to the workforce; it is also to ensure that they are good humans, capable of getting along with one another and showing empathy, support and love to those in need. We needn't agree with all those who cross our path, and, as such, skills in conflict resolution and emotional intelligence are without a doubt some of the most important skills that we need to thrive in society today. Adopting an educative approach to behaviour management allows us to teach and model skills such as these.

Bringing the focus back to learning

When I mapped out the chapters you'll read in book I thought deeply about how I would position student misbehaviour in these pages. I had to critically challenge my own thinking in relation to how best to represent the behaviours that are considered to be unfavourable to a positive learning environment. There are many terms I could have used: 'inappropriate behaviour', 'disruptive behaviour' and 'misbehaviour', to name a few. It was, initially, difficult to settle on a term because some undesirable behaviours are *not* disruptive. For example, a student sitting at the back of the class playing games on their iPad might not be disrupting others in the class, but it is an undesirable behaviour in the sense that it is not focused on learning. In the end, I settled on the term 'off-task behaviour'. I use the term 'off-task behaviour' to represent the most common low-level behaviours that we experience in classrooms such as talking out of turn, low levels of attention, idleness, hindering others and not following (reasonable) instructions directed towards enhancing learning. These low-level behaviours divert attention away from teaching and learning and are the main challenges that teachers face in in Australian classrooms (OECD, 2023; Paramita et al., 2020).

Opting to use 'off-task behaviour' as an all-encompassing umbrella term helps us to change the narrative on how we approach behaviour education in schools. At the end of the day, our core focus as teachers is teaching, and if students are engaging in behaviours that detract from their own or others' learning, we must bring the focus back to being on-task with learning. This is contextual and will look different for each student. For example, some students will need more assistance and co-regulation than others.

When you encounter a student engaging in off-task behaviour, I implore you to change the narrative in your head with one simple word: *opportunity*. You have the power to change the narrative on education in Australia in and through your actions as you adopt a behaviour education perspective in your classrooms. It is a fantastic profession and we can impact students' learning well beyond test scores. We have the opportunity to influence the social fabric in which we are all a part. Let's educate our students on how to be good to each other and how to ask for help in situations where they need it the most.

Let's be brave and see students' off-task behaviours not as a burden to manage but as an opportunity to fulfill the central role of a school: to educate.

How to use this book

I have written this book to support teachers at all stages of their career, and also for school leaders. Part I is centred around creating a culture of support as part of a behaviour education approach in schools. Part II is focused on preventative and in-the-moment behaviour management practices that can assist teachers to lead positive classrooms. It also includes a whole-school behaviour education model.

Individual teachers can of course adopt the key messages in this book, but it will be more powerful if the entire school community does so. (Chapter 5 provides an example framework to help support this.) It is my hope that this book might be given to teachers at the start of the school year and that it provides a basis for teacher-led professional learning, creating a common language around how to approach off-task behaviours in schools. If this happens, I have done my job well.

I wanted to make this book as practical as possible. It includes exemplar conversational scripts, worked examples of different strategies and approaches, and reflection activities at the end of each chapter. I understand that, in the busyness and practicalities of your work, you may find it difficult to access research, so I have discussed relevant research in an accessible manner throughout. The research that I have cited is by no means exhaustive, and I encourage you to do some further reading on the topics that interest you.

As you read the book and engage with the chapter reflections it is essential that you take time to pause and reflect. To support you with this, the chapter reflections serve four purposes:

1. They provide some structure around the book and ensure that before you move to the next chapter you are given the opportunity to consider your learnings.
2. They are designed in a way that honours professional learning communities and the power of reflective collaborative practice with others.
3. They assist in challenging your assumptions.
4. They provide you the opportunity to think about the implications of what you've read for your own practice.

To begin this process of reflection, I encourage you to engage with the following activity.

On the following page you will see a blank box. There is nothing special about this box – yet. This is your box. Your space. It is your beginning. I would like you to take the time right now to detail whatever comes to mind before you embark on the journey of reading this book. This may be a reflection about what you are hoping to achieve during this school year. It may be what you are most challenged by currently with a particular student or class. It could be a reflection on what your ideal classroom looks like and why. You could even draw a representation of this. You can do whatever you like in this section, as it is a space to acknowledge where you are at this point in time.

Once you finish this book, or perhaps after you have put some of the strategies I've written about into practice, I want you to return to this page often. This initial reflection will serve as a powerful reminder of how far you have come with your behaviour education practice.

PART I

EVERYTHING IS RELATIONSHIP

'Alone we can do so little; together we can do so much.' – Helen Keller

The creator of the geodesic dome, Buckminster Fuller, once said, 'Relationships are everything and everything is relationship.' Fuller saw the world and everything in it as a whole – an intricate tapestry where everything is connected to everything else. Importantly, he believed that the relationships between things are just as important as the things themselves. This may sound pretty self-explanatory, but take a moment to really let that sink in – *everything is relationship*. Philosophically, it is a remarkable paradox to reflect upon. We are at the same time 'self' and 'the world'. If I were to leverage the work of German philosopher Martin Heidegger from a phenomenological perspective, our experience of *being* only emerges through our participation in relationships. This view sees the wholeness of life as a process that comes into existence only when all living beings interact with one another. Extraordinary, isn't it? You and I may not have met and perhaps we never will. Yet, because I have typed these words and you are now reading them, we simultaneously create and experience life in and through each other. I don't know about you, but I feel a certain sense of humanity knowing that you and I are here in this moment, together.

Expanding upon this further is the concept of Ubuntu, which has its roots in humanist African philosophy. The guiding principle of Ubuntu is simple: a person is a person through other persons. It is a way of living that is premised by the fact that 'I am' only because 'we are'. It recognises that community is a core building block of society. Aristotle's well-known maxim, 'The whole is greater than the sum of its parts', also reflects this.

If I were to hand you all the components of a car, they would have no movement value unless they were combined to create a car. Most importantly, you would more than likely have to rely on relationships with others in order to build the car in the first place. Let's now take that philosophical knowledge and apply it back to Fuller's geodesic dome – a hemispherical, thin-shell structure based on geodesic polyhedron. In simpler terms, it's a dome made of many interconnected triangles. The triangular elements in a geodesic dome are formed in such a way that they distribute the stress and load throughout the entire structure, ensuring that it can withstand heavy loads. Every triangle relies on every other triangle to ensure that the structure doesn't collapse in on itself. The whole of the structure is greater than the sum of the individual triangles that comprise it.

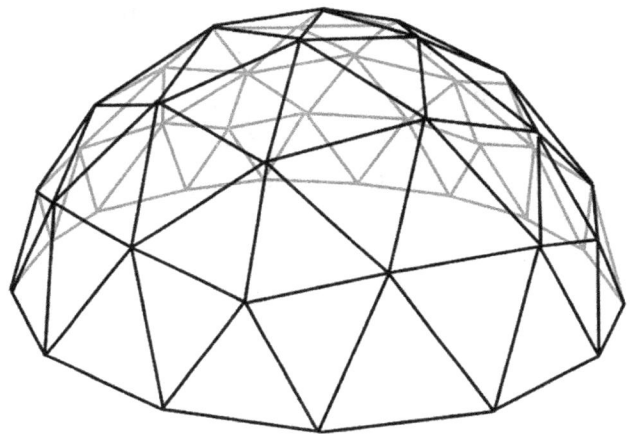

Interestingly, many greenhouses make use of geodesic domes. The structure maximises sunlight and interior space, ensuring even temperature inside the dome and affording the plants inside the opportunity to grow to their full potential. We would do well to visualise supporting students with behaviour education in much the same way.

A central message within this book is that behaviour education *is* a geodesic dome. For all the ways that you, the teacher, can redirect off-task behaviour in the classroom, there really is no substitute for building a geodesic dome around students to support them with their learning and wellbeing. We know that it takes a village to raise a child, and sometimes it feels like a whole metropolis is needed if you have 'that' Year 9 class for the last period on a Friday afternoon. We must lean in to the philosophy of Ubuntu and build positive relationships with key stakeholders, including our students themselves, so that strong geodesic domes are formed, allowing for behaviour education to occur.

I don't mean to sound evangelical with this metaphor, and I recognise that there are certain structural and systemic pressures that make this difficult to achieve. However, if I was to stress one thing that I have learnt across the multiple student management roles that I have had in schools, it's this: successful behaviour education is premised on positive relationships with many. I am, because we are.

Part I of this book is divided into three chapters: Chapter 1 discusses how to build referent power with students through high-growth relationships; Chapter 2 adopts an ecological perspective on behaviour education and explores how to leverage the support of colleagues and parents/guardians; and Chapter 3 considers a trauma-informed pedagogical approach to behaviour education. These chapters provide a platform for teachers to approach behaviour education in much the same way as building a geodesic dome – working *with* and *alongside* students and their immediate circles in holistic and supportive ways.

CHAPTER 1

BUILDING REFERENT POWER THROUGH HIGH-GROWTH RELATIONSHIPS

*'The strength of the team is each individual member.
The strength of each member is the team.' – Phil Jackson*

Building and maintaining positive relationships with students is central to behaviour education. Without positive relationships, the wrong forms of power are relied upon to influence and correct students' off-task behaviours – notably coercive techniques that leverage fear as the driver of influence. As we move to take the more holistic approach of behaviour education, we must avoid threats-based approaches that (re)enforce cycles of perpetual discipline. As Henry Ford, founder of Ford Motor Company, said, 'Coming together is a beginning, staying together is progress, and working together is success.' The success of behaviour education relies heavily on teachers and students working together, developing prosocial behaviours and positive dispositions to learning through a focused collaborative effort.

This chapter starts off by exploring different types of social power and explains how each relates to the teacher-student relationship. Next, we'll look at a framework for building referent power with students through high-growth relationships, highlighting the importance of high expectations and high care. The chapter concludes with practical strategies that teachers can employ to establish purposeful connections with students.

Chapter learning intentions

By the end of this chapter, you will be able to:

- understand the different forms of social power
- use strategies to purposefully connect with students
- develop referent power with students through high-growth relationships
- reflect on and explore the implications for your own classroom practice.

Understanding power

We must first acknowledge that any attempt to change a student's behaviour is an act of power. I think of it in terms of Newton's principle of inertia; that is, an object will continue in its current motion until some force causes its speed or direction to change. That force is your actions as the teacher in the classroom.

How we exercise or experience power, though, is not considered to be universal. In the 1950s, social psychologists John French and Bertram Raven studied the complex nature of social power, suggesting that it is 'pervasive, complex, and often disguised in our society' (French & Raven, 1959). They defined power in terms of its influence on a person, which is produced by another social agent and can be a person, a role, a norm, a group or a part of a group. Power is the primary conduit used to achieve desired results or compliance from another. French and Raven determined that there were five bases of power: reward, coercive, legitimate, referent and expert. Later work from Raven (1965) added a sixth base of power: informational. An explanation of these bases of power, and how they relate to the teacher-student relationship in the domain of behaviour education, is provided in Table 1.1.

Table 1.1: The six bases of power as they relate to the domain of behaviour education

	Definition	Application
Reward power	Power based on the ability to reward. The strength of the power increases with the magnitude of the reward that a person believes another person can provide.	The teacher provides a student with reward or recognition for appropriate behaviour and/or outcomes. This can be tangible, experiential or verbal.
Coercive power	Similar to reward power in that it involves a person's ability to manipulate outcomes. The difference, though, is that coercive power stems from the expectation that a person will be punished if they fail to conform to the influence attempt.	The teacher uses threats that operate on students' desire to avoid punishment for off-task behaviour, e.g. 'Stop doing that or you will get a detention.'
Legitimate power	Power that stems from a person's internalised values which dictate that another person has a legitimate right to influence them, while also having an obligation to accept this influence.	Once qualified, teachers have legitimacy placed upon them by society to educate young people, so the teacher has a tacitly implied form of legitimate power in schools.
Referent power	Referent power is built through relationships and involves the identification of a person with another person – a feeling of oneness. Referent power is based on the respect and admiration an individual has earnt from others over time.	Both the student and the teacher place their trust and confidence in one another, and they seek to form and maintain a positive teacher-student relationship.

	Definition	Application
Expert power	The strength of expert power varies with the extent of the knowledge or perception a person attributes to another person in a given area.	A student believes that the teacher is an expert in their field, and that they will gain knowledge and/or skills in and through learning experiences provided by the teacher.
Informational power	The ability of a person to influence another person through the resource of information, which is strongly linked to the notion of persuasion.	The teacher presents, or withholds, certain forms of information to alter a student's behaviour.

ADAPTED FROM FRENCH & RAVEN, 1959 AND RAVEN (1965).

In their study of over 5000 students' perceptions of classroom discipline strategies in Australia, Israel and China, Lewis et al. (2005) found that Australian teachers' unwillingness to empower students in the behaviour management decision-making process was due to the 'lower levels of unconditional respect they are likely to receive from students, and the reduced levels of support parents provide [teachers]'. This, according to Lewis et al. (2005), signifies that Australian teachers have relatively lower levels of legitimate power, and, as such, seek to rely on more coercive power to manage their classrooms.

Of the bases of power listed in Table 1.1, the use of coercive power is one that warrants extreme scrutiny. We have long moved on from using threats of punishment to correct behaviour, and I hope that this book serves as a guide in which to distance ourselves from a threats-based approach as a first action. If a student's off-task behaviour continues and a more scaled response is required, there is certainly a need to remind them of reasonable and logical consequences if the behaviour continues (e.g. second warning, movement, conversation after class, phone call home). However, this should be delivered in a respectful way rather than as a threat.

The other bases of power are considered relatively positive by both the influencee and influencer (Erchul & Raven, 1997; Kovach, 2020). For example, a whole-school behaviour support system might include a reward structure, and the teacher might distribute rewards for desired behaviour shown by a student or a class (e.g. a token system, excursions, a whole-class celebration). Related to expert power, as a teacher enhances their pedagogical content knowledge through professional learning, they build their expertise in a subject area and this may enhance students' perceptions of the teacher's ability to positively influence their learning.

Some power bases have been shown to have a greater influence than others. Leveraging knowledge drawn from Ryan and Deci's (2017) self-determination theory, Peyton et al. (2018) explored relationships between followers' perceptions of their leader's use of various forms of power, followers' self-reported motivational outlooks and followers' favourable work intentions. The authors found that followers' perceptions of *hard power* use by their leaders (reward, coercive and legitimate power) were often related to higher levels of sub-optimal motivation in followers. In contrast to this, followers who felt that their leaders used *soft power* (expert, referent and informational power) often experienced higher levels of optimal intrinsic motivation to engage with favourable work intentions. Although the findings from this study were drawn from working professionals, I have seen much the same results when I have worked with teachers as a behaviour education mentor and critical friend. When I have observed 'hard classes' as part of this work, there has almost always been a correlation between the class descending into chaos and the teacher drawing upon *hard power* to correct behaviour, especially when it has been of a coercive nature. The key takeaway here is that successful behaviour education builds students' *intrinsic motivation* to engage in desired behaviours through bases of power that promote them to occur.

Tauber's (1986) analysis of French and Raven's power bases details how the influence of reward and legitimate power bases diminishes over time in school settings. Reward power becomes ineffective as soon as the student perceives that the teacher is no longer able to provide desired rewards, or is no longer seen as the sole entity from which rewards come (e.g. because they have a growing circle of friends and the desire for social recognition, part-time employment, changing views on what is rewarding). Over the last decades, Edward Deci and colleagues have conducted much research to determine the effects of external rewards on intrinsic motivation. What they have constantly found is that the provision of external rewards actually decreases a person's intrinsic motivation to engage in a specific behaviour (Deci et al., 1999, 2001; Deci & Ryan, 1985; Ryan & Deci, 2017). For reward power to be most effective as a behaviour management strategy, it must relate to the acknowledgement of desired behaviours or dispositions (e.g. through behaviour-specific praise, which is discussed in Chapter 4).

Legitimate power ceases when the student stops accepting the rights of a teacher's position, or, more commonly, when the teacher is perceived to overstep the boundaries of the legitimate power granted to them. Michel Foucault, the French postmodernist, discusses the legitimacy of power in his 1977 book, *Discipline and Punish*. A central theme in much of Foucault's writing is how knowledge and power are inextricably linked. Power, according to Foucault, is everywhere and it is embodied in discourse, knowledge and 'regimes of truth' (Foucault, 1977). Foucault argued that legitimate power is constituted as truth – accepted through forms of knowledge largely garnered from scientific understanding – and this is open to forms of resistance. When students think critically about the purpose of education (which is a good thing), they can challenge the legitimacy of the teacher's role. Expert power then becomes less about the teacher being the giver of all knowledge, and more about the learning experiences they provide. This is no more evident than in the current technology-driven epoch in which we all live, where students are able to access an endless amount of knowledge from the palm of their hand. This, too, is why informational power is a shaky ledge on which to stand as a base of power to influence students' behaviour.

This leaves us with referent power – the power of relationships, and a feeling of oneness. Although referent power is dependent upon student perceptions, it is not as easily eroded as the other power bases, and it is the engine room of successful behaviour education.

This power base creates a sense of unity. It promotes strong working relationships, and is built upon a foundation of trust and democracy. It allows for influence (e.g. behaviour correction) to occur through respect and dialogue. With referent power, you transform yourself from a manager of classrooms to a *leader* of classrooms, and you adopt a behaviour education mindset.

However, referent power is not granted automatically. It has to be cultivated and maintained. It is not commanded, it is earnt. Some teachers find this easier than others, and that is just the nature of relationship-building. Here's the hard truth: in some schools it is more difficult to build referent power with students than it is in others.

Not all schools are the same

I want to reiterate this very firmly: all young people can learn and achieve great things in life with the right structures and supports behind them. Good behaviour management takes a high level of commitment from all those in a school, including the students themselves. As you will see in Chapter 5, consistency is key to successfully implementing an educative approach to behaviour management in schools. It is hard work and there are no shortcuts. For some schools, though, behaviour management is a much harder task.

Not all school communities share the same demographics and socioeconomic status. Some schools benefit from families who provide their children with stable home environments where education has been valued. This valuing of education is passed down to the young people who walk through the school gates each day – the silver spoon of opportunity. There will still be behaviour management in these schools, but off-task behaviours might be easily dealt with in the moment. For other schools, especially those with a higher proportion of students from socioeconomically disadvantaged backgrounds or who have experienced dislocation or trauma, behaviour in the classroom will undoubtably look different.

We have to remember that some students' backpacks are heavier than others. They carry the weight of their experiences, and it is much more difficult to run the race of schooling when you are lugging around a

50 kilogram backpack when the people next to you (in your school) or on other fields (other schools) are not. What remains consistent, though, is the focus on building positive relationships with students and ensuring that they succeed, no matter what their backgrounds are. Every child deserves a champion who believes in them and stands in their corner, cheering them on to be their very best. In some instances, you may have to help them carry their backpack and learn how to make it lighter (e.g. self-regulation through co-regulation).

Water the orchard

In some schools, teachers will have to work ten times harder to build referent power with students, especially for those who may have never had a trustworthy and reliable adult in their lives. I want to encourage you to never give up, even when things get hard and you experience pushback from students. Think of it like planting a fruit tree: you prepare the soil, plant the young tree and fertilise and water it to ensure that it grows. It takes some time for the tree to bear fruit; there may be certain seasons where fruit doesn't grow, while others bring an abundant harvest. Building referent power is like compound interest – *do the work, and then let the work do the work*. One fruit tree may just grow into an orchard, and you will look back and marvel at what you and your students have grown together.

My question for you all, and perhaps one you might share with others in your school, is: *are you watering your orchard?* It is an apt metaphor for building referent power with students. Watering the orchard together with your students (relationships) yields fruit (learning and wellbeing outcomes). When they're not watered, our fruit trees dry up and wither. Then what happens if there is a spot fire? The fruit trees are so dry that they can act as tinder and cause a bushfire. We then spend much of our time and energy on putting out the fire instead of focusing on the growth of the tree and its potential yield.

Not all schools and students share the same conditions; some students have sprinkler systems while others are relying on a leaky watering can. Whatever the conditions you find yourself working in, it is important to meet each student at their point of need to find ways to best water the orchard, together.

The next section of the book provides a framework for creating orchards with students. Perhaps we can think of the framework as a plot of land for you to start planting young fruit trees. This plot of land is premised around building referent power with students by developing high-growth relationships with them.

An overview of the referent power framework

You now know that building referent power should form the basis of your approach to behaviour education, but how exactly do you build referent power?

Before we delve into the practical strategies that you can employ, we first must understand the two elements that facilitate building referent power with students: high expectations for learning, and high care. Once you understand these two elements and how they coalesce it becomes easier to focus on developing positive and meaningful connections with students so that they flourish as learners, and you flourish as a practitioner. This is similar to an approach I encountered during my time with Victoria Police – create the highest possible operating standards and enact them in a manner that simultaneously supports and strengthens everyone's ability to work together successfully within those standards.

The framework for building referent power with students through high-growth relationships (Figure 1.1) is underpinned by relational theory (Cait, 2016; Downie & Llewellyn, 2011), which posits that human existence is fundamentally formed in and through the relationships we have with others. Furthermore, the two elements of the framework are supported by the findings of Gregory et al. (2010b). In the study, the authors investigated the effects of consistent and fair school discipline (structure) and availability of caring adults (support) on school climate in 290 high schools in Virginia, the United States. In the study, it was found that schools that operated with high levels of structure and support were thought of as safe by students and were associated with less bullying and victimisation (e.g. abusive remarks and being physically attacked and injured). These findings suggest that behaviour management practices should not be polarised into a 'tough at all costs' versus 'wrap them up in cotton wool' debate, because both structure and support contribute to a positive school environment for students. Indeed, in closing their analysis, Gregory et al. (2010b) note: 'Just as many adolescents benefit from authoritative parenting in their home, students may benefit from a similarly authoritative environment in their school.' Simply, we must lead for behaviour.

The framework I present anchors teachers' thinking on having high expectations for, and showing high care towards, all students in a classroom. Let's now take a look at the elements of the framework as well as the different types of relationships that exist within it.

Figure 1.1: A framework for building referent power with students through high-growth relationships

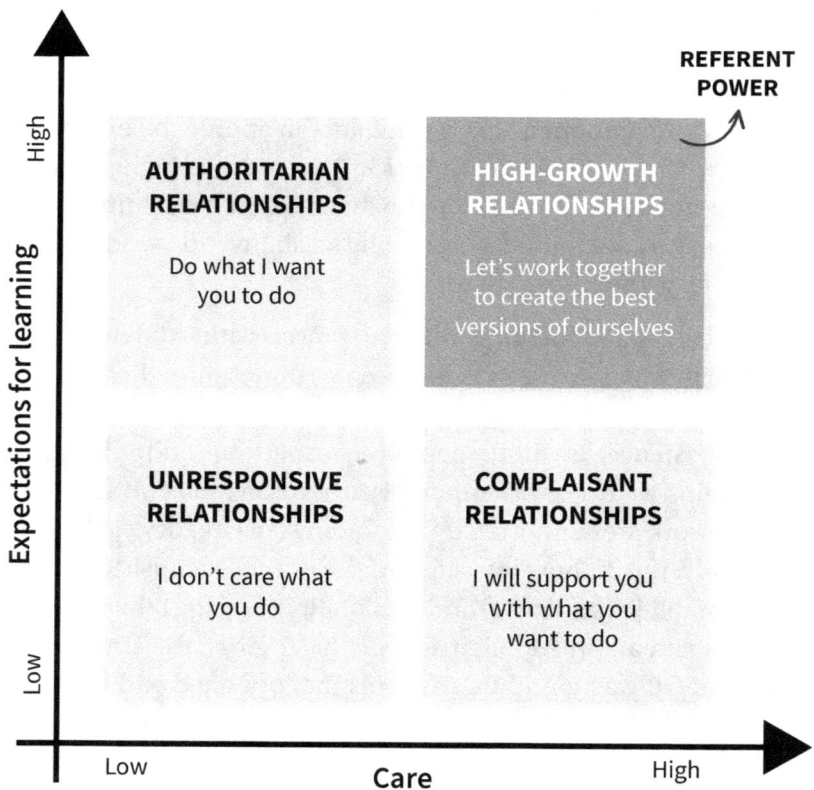

Elements of the framework

Expectations for learning (the structure)

Teachers' expectations for students' achievement are an important influence on students' learning (Hattie, 2008, 2023). Different levels of expectations lead to different instructional practices and pedagogical interventions. For example, a teacher who has low achievement expectations for a particular student may present that student with less cognitively demanding learning experiences. The teacher may also spend more time repeating information rather than extending the student's learning, and they may also accept substandard work that shows that minimal learning has occurred. Having low expectations establishes an acceptance of low-level learning experiences in the classroom, and this can lead to off-task behaviour stemming from boredom and a lack of cognitive stimulation.

When a teacher's expectations for student achievement increases, their instructional practices change to allow students to engage in more challenging learning within their 'zone of proximal development' (Vygotsky, 1978). Lev Vygotsky, the Russian psychologist best known for his sociocultural theory, defined the zone of proximal development as 'the distance between the actual developmental level as determined by independent problem solving and the level of potential development as determined through problem solving under adult guidance, or in collaboration with more capable peers' (Vygotsky, 1978). This 'Goldilocks zone' is where the learning experience presented is neither too hard nor too easy. It's the space in which learning growth is likely to occur. The provision of differentiated learning experiences within a student's zone of proximal development allows a teacher to foster positive dispositions to learning as part of the behaviour education approach they adopt in their classroom.

Care (the support)

Great teachers care about their students. They want them to succeed and are committed to helping them achieve their learning goals. Great teachers also care about their students' happiness, wellbeing, sense of belonging and life beyond the classroom. They show they care by explicitly celebrating milestones and achievements with their students.

An essential component of caring is empathetic listening, which is the process of building rapport with the person speaking to understand how they are feeling. A teacher does this when they put themselves into a student's shoes, seeking to understand how they view the world. Stephen Covey, author of *The 7 Habits of Highly Effective People*, explained that the biggest communication problem is that we don't listen to understand – we listen to reply. Empathetic listening is *listening to understand*, and it is a core component of engaging in dialogue with students.

It is important to distinguish between dialogue and discussion, as the two are different and yield different results. Discussion is about advocating viewpoints and challenging those of others. Dialogue, on the other hand, is about finding a shared connection with another – listening, understanding and building a collective narrative. Paulo Freire, a Brazilian philosopher and educator, spoke at length about the importance of engaging in dialogue with others as a practice of freedom in his 1970 book, *Pedagogy of the Oppressed*. In the book, Freire commented: 'Leaders who do not act dialogically, but insist on imposing their decisions, do not organise the people – they manipulate them. They do not liberate, nor are they liberated: they oppress' (Freire, 1970). I would argue that the goal of behaviour education is the antithesis of oppression; it is to engage in dialogue with students as an act of freedom. Freire described five practices that he believed important as part of the dialogical process: engaging in humility, hope, faith, love and critical thinking. These five practices underpin the process of engaging in dialogue with students in and through the adoption of a behaviour education approach in schools.

Engaging in dialogue with students is as much a mindset as it is a practice of care. Doing so allows us to find reasonable and achievable solutions to problems together with our students. Dialogue offers teachers a way to build referent power with students by displaying interpersonal skills that inspire mutual confidence, trust and respect. Engaging in dialogue with students also provides the scaffolds required for learning, whether that be academically or behaviourally. Simply put, engaging in dialogue shows students that we care about them: their opinions, their values and their ideas.

The different relationships within the framework

Unresponsive relationships

Unresponsive relationships are characterised by low expectations for learning and low care. The message to students is: 'I don't care what you do.' For me, this is a scary classroom to walk into as a mentor and critical friend. There is no direction provided in the lesson and there is very little authentic engagement between the teacher and the student. Imagine students climbing on furniture and throwing shoes at one another while the teacher sits at the front of the class using their computer and telling the students to be quiet (yes, I have seen this). Perhaps a less dramatic visualisation is the teacher handing out a stock- standard, low-level worksheet to students while sitting at the front of the class and not engaging in any pedagogical action. Unresponsive relationships invite students to engage in off-task behaviour through boredom and a lack of support.

Authoritarian relationships

Authoritarian relationships are characterised by high expectations for learning and low care. The message to students is: 'Do what I want you to do.' I have found that teachers who rely on authoritarian relationships generally leverage legitimate and coercive power to manage students' off-task behaviour. Expectations for students' learning may be high, but they might be limited to performance-based outcomes such as test scores rather than allowing the time and space for students to explore key concepts with one another in different contexts. The desire to engage in dialogue with students is limited or non-existent. It is a one-way street and the students' thoughts, feelings and opinions are not recognised. Authoritarian relationships invite students to engage in off-task behaviour through a desire to seek agency and challenge authority.

Complaisant relationships

Complaisant relationships are characterised by high care and low expectations for learning. The message to students is: 'I am here to support you with what you want to do.' While complaisant relationships might seek to acknowledge students' voices and agency, this might also be at the expense of having high expectations for students' learning. Complaisant relationships invite students to engage in off-task behaviour through a lack of structure and appropriate boundaries in the classroom.

High-growth relationships

High-growth relationships are characterised by high care and high expectations for learning, and this is a reciprocal influence between the teacher and the student. The message to students is: 'Let's work together to create the best versions of ourselves.' Teamwork and collaboration are the core focuses of high-growth relationships between teachers and students. Charles Darwin, British naturalist and father of evolutionary theory, once said, 'It is the long history of humankind (and animal kind, too) that those who learned to collaborate and improvise most effectively have prevailed.' Darwin spent many years developing his famous evolution theory. During those years, he realised that the success of many species, including humans, was reliant on collaboration and teamwork to grow and evolve. This tenet is a feature of high-growth relationships: not just the evolution of our students, but also of ourselves. We grow and evolve as learners, teachers *and* humans.

If I were to ask you about *your* most impactful teacher, what would you say about them? What is one word that comes to mind? Take a moment to really think about it. For me, the word that comes to mind is 'mentor'. My most memorable teacher was a mentor, not just in school but in life. Whenever I went off track, which was quite often, the way he spoke to me was always compassionate, respectful and solution-focused. I was able to provide honest feedback to him about how I was feeling and what I needed to better connect with what was happening in the classroom, and he *genuinely* listened. Not once did I ever feel a sense of punishment. Consequences came, sure – but they were always reasonable and just.

This teacher challenged me to constantly be a better version of myself, and there was never any judgement while I learnt how to navigate my teenage years. He was exactly the person I needed at that stage of my life, and in many ways, I have modelled myself as a teacher off his practices. He had high expectations for me not only as a learner, but as a human. He was the kind of teacher who showed care towards his students by engaging in genuine dialogue *with* and *alongside* them. To be honest, I was much better behaved in his class than in others, and that is because of the practices he enacted: he had high expectations for every student, he developed classroom routines and structures, he provided engaging learning experiences, he used differentiated instruction, he was responsive to students' feedback to better his own practice, he showed humility and vulnerability, and he valued dialogue with his students. As a result, he was able to build and maintain referent power with his students through meaningful connections – that is, high-growth relationships.

So far in this chapter we have seen that referent power is based on collaboration and influence and is less about command and control. It is built through high-growth relationships and can inspire both teachers and students to work towards a common goal. It relies on developing and enacting interpersonal skills that build confidence, trust and respect. Let's now take a look at some practical strategies that you can use to build referent power with your students.

Toolkit: Building referent power with students

Start with why

I write this book through the lens of a teacher who has been there on the ground, learning relationship-building skills as I go. I would love to tell you that the key to building referent power with students is simple, but I would be lying. The hard truth is that it's bloody hard. Relationship-building with students takes time, it is incredibly contextual, and the relationships need constant maintenance – there is no silver bullet. However, I can tell you with much certainty that having high expectations and showing high care toward students is the key to building referent power with them.

At times, though, things haven't gone to plan no matter how hard I have tried. I have never given up because I truly believe that each and every student that crosses my path deserves the best version of me. Sometimes, I have had to come back to my *why* as a teacher to remind me to keep trying and I urge you to do the same. Simon Sinek, author of *Start with Why: How Great Leaders Inspire Everyone to Action*, argues that every action should start with *why*. Your *why* is your purpose – your driving cause – and what you believe to be most important.

Sinek explains that creating a *why* statement enables you to cement a higher purpose, which then acts as a source of inspiration for all that you do – the *how* and the *what*. For me, my *why* statement is: *To support young people to become confident, creative and critical thinkers who value supporting others in the name of positive social transformation.* From this, my *how* is through high expectations and high care for students' learning and behaviour. My *what* is, essentially, high-quality pedagogy and behaviour education strategies, delivered in an environment of dialogue, trust and respect.

Take a moment now to write down your *why* and think deeply about your purpose as a teacher. You may need to come back to this page at times to remind you of your higher purpose in education.

Your *why* statement …

Your how:

Your what:

Next, establish purposeful connections

I have learnt that in order to build referent power with students, especially those who display more challenging behaviours, we must first devote time to establishing *purposeful connections* with them. A purposeful connection is one where both parties benefit from knowing each other. The connection is not transactional in the sense that once the parties know each other, either the teacher or the student does something for the other in the hope that they will get something in return. Rather, the connection is transformational, whereby future evolution of the relationship occurs because both parties want it to. It is, essentially, the primary strategy of knowing your students, having them know you and finding common ground. As a process, it involves finding an opportunity to connect, choosing a strategy to connect and then acting upon that strategy (Figure 1.2).

Figure 1.2: The process of making purposeful connections with students

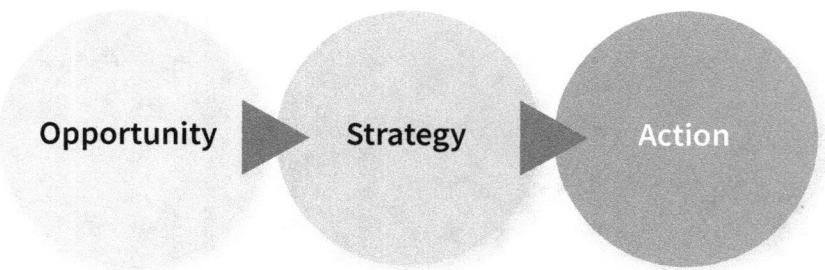

The next section details some practical strategies that you can use to establish purposeful connections with students, divided into three primary and two secondary, but affiliated, strategies. See Table 1.2 for an overview.

Table 1.2: Overview of strategies to build purposeful connections with students

Purposeful connections	Primary goal	Know your students, have them know you and find common ground		
	Primary strategies	Learner snapshot	Surveys and interviews	Life story narrative presentation
	Secondary strategies	The 2 × 10 strategy	Community embeddedness	

Know your students, have them know you and find common ground

Getting to know a student as a whole person instead of just by their academic performance will go a long way towards building referent power with them. Indeed, this is recognised as Strategy 1 in the Department of Education Victoria's *High Impact Wellbeing Strategies* (Allen et al., 2022) and Standard 1 in the Australian Institute of Teaching and School Leadership's *Professional Standards for Teachers* (AITSL, 2017). An important initial focus is learning students' names. It is a remarkably simple, yet extremely effective, strategy to employ when you have a new class. I am constantly amazed at just how much impact referring to a student by their name has on building referent power. When I was a year level coordinator, I remember talking to a student who had just been exited from class about what the antecedent to the off-task behaviour was. He said to me, 'She doesn't even know my name. I'm Michael but she keeps calling me Matthew and it's Term 2. She should know my name by now. It's annoying! I think she just does it to annoy me.' Once we rectified this issue with the teacher through a group restorative conversation together, things started to go a lot smoother in the class between the teacher and that student. It was a simple fix with a huge effect.

Showing students that you want to know things about them highlights that you care deeply about them not only as a student, but also as a human. Have you ever met a student who loves video games and could spend hours talking about them? What about a student who spends their whole weekend playing and watching footy? Take advantage of these interests and purposefully spend time talking to the student about them. What is it that the student loves about that particular hobby or interest? Become a learner yourself and ask the student questions about what is that they love to do. Some of the best personal learning I have done in schools has come from adopting a curious mindset and purposefully seeking moments to learn more about students' interests. I have learnt all about coding and the game Minecraft by taking the time to talk to students and showing genuine interest in their interests. I've then been able to transfer that knowledge into designing engaging lessons for those students, while also creating space for students to lead aspects of the lesson as knowledgeable experts.

Pedagogically, it is of great value to connect students' interests to the learning activities they are doing in class. For example, If you are covering the concept of Pythagorean theorem in Mathematics, and you know that members of the class have a passion for building and construction, then leverage that passion. Focus on designing learning experiences for the student so that you can transfer the concept of Pythagorean theorem to how a carpenter builds different-angled roofs depending upon the roof height and width of the frame, or how a concreter checks the squareness of their set-up in preparation to pour a house slab. When you know your students, and you have high expectations for them, you can seek ways to connect the curriculum to their interests so that deep and meaningful learning occurs. This is, simply, good teaching.

I've also championed students getting to know me and who I am outside of the classroom. I have a whole range of interests that I think are pretty cool – writing books is now one of them. There is a certain sense of vulnerability in letting students into your life, but it is an exceptional way for them to connect with you. It helps them realise that we are all in this crazy game of life together – Ubuntu. For example, I love footy and I use that interest to connect with students who like the sport, too. When Collingwood loses a game on the weekend, the students have a grand old time letting me know about it and just how much they lost by. We all have a laugh and we bond over a mutual focus point. It also allows for humour to come into the relationship-building process, which, to me, is gold.

Mirroring, which I define as the practice of bonding with students over a mutual interest, is one of the most powerful practices that you can employ. Not only is it the process of finding common ground with a student, but it is also about letting them know that the common ground you share is important to you. When I have coached staff on how to build high-growth relationships with students who display more challenging behaviours, I have often heard, 'But I do know that student!' and my response is almost always, 'Yes. But what does that student *know about you*?'.

Let's take a look at three primary strategies you can use to get to know your students and have them get to know you. We'll follow this with two secondary strategies.

Primary strategies

Learner snapshot

This activity involves students creating a snapshot of themselves as a learner, allowing you to open up space for dialogue on how best to support them in the learning journey. You can also use the students' snapshots to engage in the process of mirroring with them.

To undertake the activity, provide the students with the prompt below:

> In this task, I would like you to create a snapshot of yourself as a learner. This can be a drawing, a multimedia presentation, a poem, song lyrics or something that can be created with classroom materials. Your snapshot should reflect five things: (1) how you see yourself as a student; (2) what you like to learn about or your passions; (3) how you feel you learn best; (4) the people or things around you that help you learn; and (5) how all the elements connect with each other.

I have often done this as a check-in activity at the start of each semester, and I keep the snapshots so that students can see how their views about themselves as learners change over time. You would be surprised at how much information you can garner from an activity such as this, and the students enjoy the creative aspect of it, too.

Surveys and interviews

At the start of the school year and for each new class, I distribute a quick survey that helps me understand more about the students. You can do this through a platform such as Google Forms, and you can mould the questions however you like. Most of my questions relate to students' passions and hobbies, and any sports, clubs or associations they are involved with. Once I have this information, I create a poster that mind maps the students' interests so that we can all see the different ways we can connect with each other in the class.

I also let the students interview me in the form of a Q&A discussion (I restrict this to several broad categories and have a precursor conversation with students so that boundaries are in place to keep the questions appropriate). I get students to work in groups to come up with questions they'd like to ask me, and then I become the interviewee and they become the interviewers. I have generally held the interview in a whole-class circle formation. From my answers, I might redirect some questions to the students in the circle: who else has read that book? Who else likes footy? Has anyone else been to London? It is a great way to find common connections with students based off your own interests.

Life story narrative presentation

This activity involves you delivering a presentation (e.g. multimedia, photo board) to students about you life. I know, it sounds daunting and it does require a high level of vulnerability. But I can wholeheartedly tell you that if you lean in to the vulnerability, it's a great way to allow the students to know you: what you like to do, what drives you, what your passions are, what you're good at, what you're not so good at but trying to learn and what your goals for the future are. It invites students to connect with you through avenues that were previously unknown to them.

In my own practice I have usually done this through a quick multimedia presentation. I've included photos of me engaging in my hobbies, my favourite books, the recycled timber furniture I have built, places in the world that I have visited and those who mean the most to me – my family and friends. I speak to these photos from a place of passion, showing students how each aspect culminates in who I am as a person – a father, a brother, a son, a friend, a teacher and a colleague. Doing so invites students to connect with me on many different levels.

I have coached teachers in how to do this and I have seen the most amazing life story narrative presentations as a result. One teacher performed a singalong campfire session in class with students, which led to the class making a song together, and it created a sense of unity in the classroom for the rest of the year. Interestingly, the students had no idea that the teacher played guitar and sang prior to the singalong. I have also seen a teacher, who was an actor outside of school, conduct an improvised theatre-like presentation in class where he brought students in as characters. The students loved it so much that the teacher often used the activity as a brain break between instruction.

Be vulnerable. Be brave. Be open. It is a great way for students to connect more deeply with you.

Secondary strategies

The 2 × 10 strategy

The 2 × 10 strategy is simple: you spend two minutes per day for 10 days in a row talking with a targeted student about an area of interest for them. American educational researcher Raymond Wlodkowski originally referred to this as the two-minute intervention. In his study, Wlodkowski highlighted the power of the *two-minute intervention*, with the results showing that the targeted students had an 85% improvement in their behaviour, which, consequently, also enhanced the behaviour of all other students in the class too (Wlodkowski, 1983).

More recently, Gragg and Collett (2023) examined teachers' perceptions of the impact of the 2 × 10 strategy on improving a targeted student's behaviour. Using the Strengths and Difficulties Questionnaire developed in 1994 by child psychiatrist Robert Goodman, the authors measured teachers' perceptions of their target students' behaviour after engaging with the 2 × 10 strategy based on five factors: conduct, emotions, hyperactivity, peer problems and prosocial behaviour. While the results of the study showed no statistically significant change in decreasing students' challenging behaviours, all of the teachers recorded a change in perception of the student, connection with the student and their understanding of the student. Gragg and Collett (2023) revealed further that the 'teachers indicated that these changes led to improvements in future communications, instructional practice, and lesson planning'. These findings posit that teachers' perceptions about a student influence how they view that student's behaviour and, importantly, how they seek to address problematic behaviour through pedagogical interventions.

The 2 × 10 strategy is not only a great way to break the ice with students, it also forms a solid foundation for high-growth relationships to flourish. The strategy also flips the narrative on how to approach our most challenging students. It may seem counterintuitive, but the students who often require the most behavioural correction in class are the ones who most need a positive and personal connection with an adult role model, such as you – their teacher. Often students behave in certain ways to let us know they are seeking, and need, a positive connection before they can, or will, focus on learning.

Here's how the 2 × 10 strategy works:

1. Choose one student with whom you would like to strengthen your relationship.
2. Make time (find an opportunity) to initiate a two-minute personal, authentic conversation with that student about something that interests them.
3. In the conversation, look for an opportunity to connect with the student through mirroring (action).
4. Repeat steps 1 to 3 for 10 days.

Here are some tips for enacting the 2 × 10 strategy:

- Keep the conversation positive and focused on student interests.
- Value student voice and don't do all the talking.
- Ask open-ended questions as follow-up questions.
- Be consistent and ensure that the conversations are had for 10 days in a row.
- Keep the momentum going after 10 days.

Community embeddedness

The last strategy offered in this chapter is that of community embeddedness, which refers to the ways in which individuals are rooted and engaged in the community where they live (Hom et al., 2017). In their study examining the positive effects of community embeddedness on job-level, social-level and organisation-level outcomes, Ng and Feldman (2014) explained that successful community embeddedness entailed factors such as *fit* and *links*. Community fit refers to 'the extent to which individuals' needs and interests are congruent with the community's environment', and community links refer to 'the number of ties individuals have with other people and activities'. As it relates to teachers, community embeddedness is the extent to which a teacher is connected to others in the community outside of school. This may be through sports, clubs, societies or any other group that engages in activities together.

In my research on successful schools in rural Victoria, Australia, I have found that teachers' and principals' high level of community embeddedness is a key feature of rural school success, with positive teacher-student relationships central to this. Across the interviews that I conducted for my doctorate study, many interviewees commonly stated phrases such as 'we all know each other here', 'we are like one big, connected family' and 'we are a safe community because everyone sees everyone outside of school'. These interconnected relationships went a long way to fostering learning environments described as safe, respectful and calm. While much is written about how to make rural schools more urban (see, for example, Roberts &

Green, 2013), we would do extremely well as an education system to learn from rural schools in relation to building positive relationships with students in and through community embeddedness.

Sometimes we need to further embed ourselves into our communities to find opportunities to purposefully connect with students and their families. You can do this by finding *fit* and then building *links*. What do your students do outside of school, and can you get involved? For example, if it is footy, how can you get involved in their local club in whatever capacity you are able to? This suggestion does, however, come with a caveat. It is not beyond me to realise the workload and work intensification that many teachers find themselves dealing with at the moment. Of course, purposefully devoting further time to community embeddedness in this way adds more workload, so it might not be a suitable strategy if you already have a lot on your plate. However, venture out into the community and you will no doubt cross paths with students and their families anyway. Look at these instances as indirect opportunities to build or enhance purposeful connections with students and their families.

Here's a personal example of how this can work. I once taught an incredibly challenging all-male Year 9 Physical Education class. It took a long time to build referent power with the group, which was made up of many students who needed extra behavioural support from me. Amongst other strategies, I approached each student with unconditional positive regard, and I experienced great success by doing so. It ended up becoming one of my favourite classes to teach.

I often took my two young boys to the local park and oval on a Sunday morning, and I had noticed that a lot of the students in my class played football in the same team when I was there. I started to watch their team play with my two boys cheering them on. At the end of the game I would listen to the coach's address, and often the students would come and say hello to me and my family. The beauty of this was that they saw me as a father and not as a teacher in these moments. I was just a normal guy chasing after his kids, ensuring they weren't eating dirt or pulling the tail of every single dog on the oval.

It was the most vulnerable I had ever been with this group of students and it paid dividends. They valued that I came down to watch their home games and explicitly told me that 'no other teacher cares about us enough to do that'. That class came to be a breeze to teach and, surprisingly, the students began to regulate their own behaviour and that of others in the class themselves. As I mentioned in the introduction to this part of the book, it was compound interest – I did the work associated with community embeddedness, and then the work did the work.

CHAPTER SUMMARY AND REFLECTION

In this chapter I detailed the different types of social power and posited that referent power is at the core of a successful behaviour education approach in schools. I discussed the importance of building high-growth relationships with students, and provided several strategies to assist in this, focusing on seeking opportunities for purposeful connection.

Take a moment now to reflect on your learning and understanding using the 4 Cs thinking tool, which is best used in dialogue with a mentor or critical friend. It will help you make connections, identify key ideas and consider the application of your learning.

- **Connections:** What connections do you draw between this chapter and your own behaviour education practice?
- **Challenge:** What do you feel the current challenges or barriers are to building high-growth relationships with your students?
- **Concepts:** What key concepts or ideas do you think are important and worth holding on to from the chapter?
- **Changes:** What changes in attitudes, thinking or action are suggested in the chapter, either for you or others?

CHAPTER 2

ENGAGING IN THE MESOSYSTEM

'No one can whistle a symphony. It takes a whole orchestra to play it.' – H.E. Luccock

To strengthen the geodesic domes that we build around students, we must work with and alongside others, both inside and outside of the school. As Apple founder Steve Jobs remarked, 'Great things in business are never done by one person: they're done by a team of people.' The same can be said for schools. When all members of a school community are working together towards the common goal of supporting students through an educative approach to behaviour management, the message to students is one of support, guidance and respect. While teacher-student interactions are at the heart of behaviour education, there are also important interactions outside of these. A successful approach to behaviour education is predicated upon teamwork and consistency, which forms the central focus of this chapter.

We'll start by discussing the seminal work of Urie Bronfenbrenner, which sets the scene for how interactions outside a child's microsystem can contribute to a successful behaviour education approach in schools. Next, we'll consider functional behaviour assessments (FBAs) and how they can be used to make sense of the function behind a student's off-task behaviour, which is often complex. The chapter concludes with information on behaviour support plans (BSPs) and the steps involved in creating, monitoring and evaluating them.

Chapter learning intentions

By the end of this chapter, you will be able to:

- understand how the work of Urie Bronfenbrenner connects to behaviour education
- conduct a functional behaviour assessment (FBA) as part of a positive behaviour support team
- develop a behaviour support plan (BSP) alongside a school leader
- reflect on and explore the implications for your own classroom practice.

An introduction to the work of Urie Bronfenbrenner

Central to behaviour education is being aware of the various factors that affect student learning, before collaborating with others to create a holistic, supportive and positive environment. This is not only in the classroom, but also in the broader school, the home and the community. The work of Russian-born American psychologist Urie Bronfenbrenner can be used as a theoretical lens in which to think more deeply about this.

The aim here is to explore how students' development, which includes learning about appropriate behaviours, hinges on a complex system of relationships. These relationships are affected on multiple levels by surrounding environments, from immediate family and school settings to broader factors such as political systems and social norms. Of course, you already know this. Much of what I present in the opening sections of this chapter is not revolutionary. But it does help to ground what we know in an established theory that has been well researched over the past decades (see, for example, Bronfenbrenner & Morris, 2006; Crawford, 2020; Hayes et al., 2017; Stanley & Kuo, 2022; Tudge, 2016).

Bronfenbrenner's theory evolved over time and can be characterised in three phases, which we'll look at in turn.

Phase one (1973-1979): development in context

Bronfenbrenner first developed his ecological systems theory in the late 1970s. What makes his theory so unique is that, unlike other psychological theories developed at the time, which studied individuals in isolation from their surroundings, Bronfenbrenner chose to pay much attention to the influence of context – that is, the development of children *in* their natural environment. Bronfenbrenner (1979) showed that the developing child exists within four interrelated systems: microsystem, mesosystem, exosystem and macrosystem (Figure 2.1). In 2005 he added a fifth system, the chronosystem, to describe the influence of time.

Figure 2.1: Bronfenbrenner's ecologoical systems theory of human development

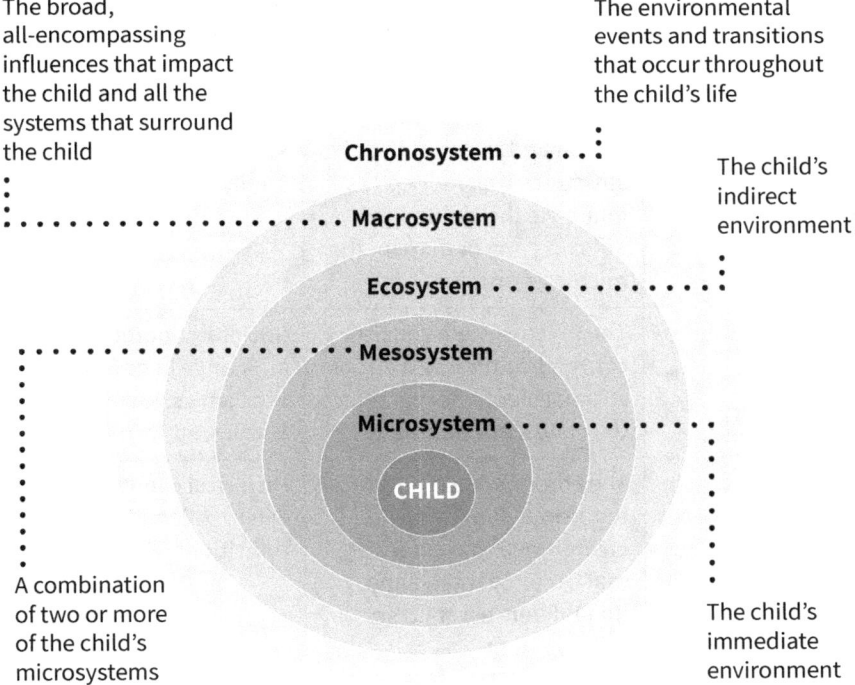

Bronfenbrenner (1977) suggested that a child develops within these nested systems of influence, which are ordered in relation to how much impact they have on a child's development. Table 2.1 explains these different systems in more detail.

Table 2.1: The five systems in Bronfenrenner's ecological systems theory of human development

	Description	Examples
1. Microsystem	The microsystem is the first level and includes things that have direct contact with the child in their immediate environment.	Family (parents and siblings), school (teachers and peers).
2. Mesosystem	The mesosystem refers to the interactions that occur between the child's microsystems. The mesosystem can be thought of as a collection of several microsystems.	School-family relationship, interactions between the child's parents and their teachers, interactions between the child and their peers.
3. Exosystem	The exosystem consists of formal and informal social structures that indirectly influence the child by affecting one or more of the microsystems.	Parents' health and employment status, family income, media.
4. Macrosystem	The macrosystem consists of broad cultural and societal elements that affect the child's development.	Societal conditions such as change in government, economics, ideology, culture, ethnicity.
5. Chronosystem	The chronosystem refers to the individual and environmental changes that occur over time and that influence a child's development.	Historical events (e.g. COVID-19), major life transitions.

ADAPTED FROM BRONFENBRENNER, 1977.

The interrelated nature of the systems means that the influence of each one is reliant and dependent upon the relationship that it has with the other systems. While the relations between systems can indirectly influence a developing child, Bronfenbrenner (1979) believed the microsystem (e.g. the teacher-student relationship) to be the system that has direct influence on a child's development.

Phase two (1980–1994): the active role of the child

During this phase, Bronfenbrenner shifted focus to recognising the active role of the child. He renamed his theory a 'bioecological model' of human development, placing greater emphasis on biological influences. Hayes et al. (2017) noted that Bronfenbrenner sought to avoid the implication that context impacts solely *on* the child, and moved his theory 'to reflect a more dynamic process whereby the context or environment impacts *with* and *through* the child's participation'. While still acknowledging development as being nested within contexts, Bronfenbrenner focused more on the *processes* that converted a child's experiences into development.

Krishnan (2010) explained that *processes* can be thought of as all the interactions (from the proximal to the distal) that a child encounters in their specific context. The mesosystem, macrosystem and exosystem represent *distal processes*, as they have an indirect influence on the child's development. *Proximal processes*, those that have a direct influence on the child's development, occur within the microsystem. Bronfenbrenner (1979) emphasised the importance of positive relationships in a child's microsystem, explaining that positive relationships are needed to adapt to, or overcome, negative environments. He believed that positive environments alone may not be sufficient to foster positive social and emotional development, and that caring relationships with others are most important.

The bioecological model also accounted for the personal dispositions and characteristics of the child, and the influence that both have on current and future development. Hayes et al. (2017) identified three distinct characteristics of the developing child (Table 2.2), which 'both shape and are shaped by experiences in context'.

Table 2.2: The three characteristics of the developing child

	Description	Elaboration
1. Active behavioural dispositions	Refers to variations in the child's motivation, persistence and temperament. Even though children might have equal access to resources, their development may differ as a function of individual personal characteristics.	Positive dispositions – including curiosity, attentiveness and the ability to defer gratification – are likely to enhance interactions and elicit responses from the environment. Negative dispositions – including distractibility, aggressive tendencies, the inability to defer gratification, and the tendency to withdraw from activity – prevent or disrupt responses from the environment.
2. Resource characteristics	Resource characteristics are not as immediately recognisable as dispositions. These include mental and emotional resources such as behaviour regulation skills, past experiences to draw upon, and cognitive ability, and material resources such as access to housing, education and a responsive parent or guardian.	The acquirement of ability, knowledge, skills and experiences that expand the range of options and sources of growth available to a child. For example, a child who has good communication skills can easily stimulate others to interact with them in dialogue. However, characteristics that limit or disrupt proximal processes include genetic inheritances such as low birthweight, physical disability and severe or persistent illness.

	Description	Elaboration
3. Demand characteristics	Demand characteristics are those qualities of the developing person that can invite or discourage reactions from the social environment, influencing the way in which proximal processes are established.	These include both passive and active characteristics such as temperament (e.g. naturally veering towards an agitated or calm nature), gender, age, physical appearance and ethnicity.

ADAPTED FROM HAYES ET AL. (2017).

Active behavioural dispositions, resource characteristics and demand characteristics are an influence on development and, concurrently, a developmental outcome (Bronfenbrenner & Morris, 2006). The process of interaction between the child and the people who coexist in their environment can be understood as 'an ongoing cycle of transformation' (Hayes et al., 2017).

A chance for reflection

Developing an understanding of processes and the three characteristics of the developing child enabled me to become a more patient, understanding and inquisitive teacher. Whenever a student was engaging in off-task behaviour in my class, I was able to step outside of the situation and *respond* rather than *react*, first seeking to understand and gain insight into that behaviour. I found myself engaging in dialogue with the student to seek answers to the following questions:

- Does the student have the required resource characteristics to be successful in this learning task?
- Have I considered differentiated learning activities to account for the student's current resource characteristics?
- Have I considered demand characteristics relating to how we work together as a class in this activity?
- How can I model and promote the desired active behavioural characteristics in a conversation with this student? Are there ways I can better connect the learning activity to the student's interests?

I recognised that there were a plethora of factors that influenced students' behaviour, and many of those factors stemmed from outside what we were actually doing in class. We may never fully know or understand students' experiences inside their own microsystems, or, secondary to this, the interactions that are occurring in their mesosystems.

Once I realised that some students may not ever have had prosocial behaviour or positive dispositions to learning modelled to them, I began to flip the narrative on how I saw off-task behaviour. My job was to be that person for them. Off-task behaviour, then, was not something to punish. Rather, it was an opportunity to educate through my own practice as a teacher.

I evolved to ask myself one simple question: 'What does this student need from me or from others right now to be successful with their learning?' Asking this question enabled me to respond in ways that aligned to the needs of the child rather than disciplinary methods of control.

Use the two prompts below to engage in reflection about your own practice:

- What connections can you make between the three characteristics of the developing child and your own experiences of managing off-task behaviours in the classroom?
- How might developing an understanding the three characteristics of the developing child enable you to change and/or adapt your approach to behaviour education?

Phase three (1994–2006): networked systems of influence through PPCT

The final phase is where Bronfenbrenner sought to capture the dynamic nature of human development in the process-person-context-time (PPCT) model of development (Table 2.3). The PPCT model of development 'drew attention to proximal processes and demonstrated how they are influenced by the context in which they occur' (Hayes et al., 2017).

Table 2.3: Components of the PPCT model of development

Process	Includes all the interactions that occur between the developing child and their surroundings, from the proximal to the distal. Bronfenbrenner (1993) suggested that proximal processes are the primary mechanisms in development, namely because it is through reciprocal and continuous interactions with the immediate environment that a child makes sense of the world.
Person	The three characteristics of the developing child operate to enhance or inhibit development. The development trajectory of a child depends upon how these characteristics interact with the child's environment.
Context	Covers all the ecological systems (Figure 2.1) and, according to Bronfenbrenner (1979, 2005), is the most critical component in understanding human development.
Time	The last component, represented by the chronosystem, is time. Bronfenbrenner (1979, 1993, 2005) explained that this incorporated both chronological time and events. For example, adolescence is a stage of life that specifically covers the period of life from 12 to 18 years of age. Events, on the other hand, refer to changes in family structure and environment, and transitions (e.g. the transition from Grade 6 to Year 7).

ADAPTED FROM BRONFENBRENNER (1979, 1993, 2005).

Implications for practice

Now that we have briefly covered Bronfenbrenner's large body of work over many decades, it's time to discuss how it relates to behaviour education, specifically the promotion of prosocial behaviours and positive dispositions to learning. When looking at Bronfenbrenner's theory of development, we see that learnt behaviour is a remarkably complex phenomenon. It is, of course, beyond our locus of control as teachers to fully account for all the different interactions that occur in and across students' ecological systems. Some of the interactions that students have will enhance their behaviour and approach to learning in class, but some will not. It is contextual and there is a plethora of forces that shape a student's willingness to engage with learning that year, that term, that day or that lesson.

Let's now look at an example of a student displaying off-task behaviour through the PPCT model (Figure 2.2).

Figure 2.2: An example of the PPCT model in relation to student behaviour

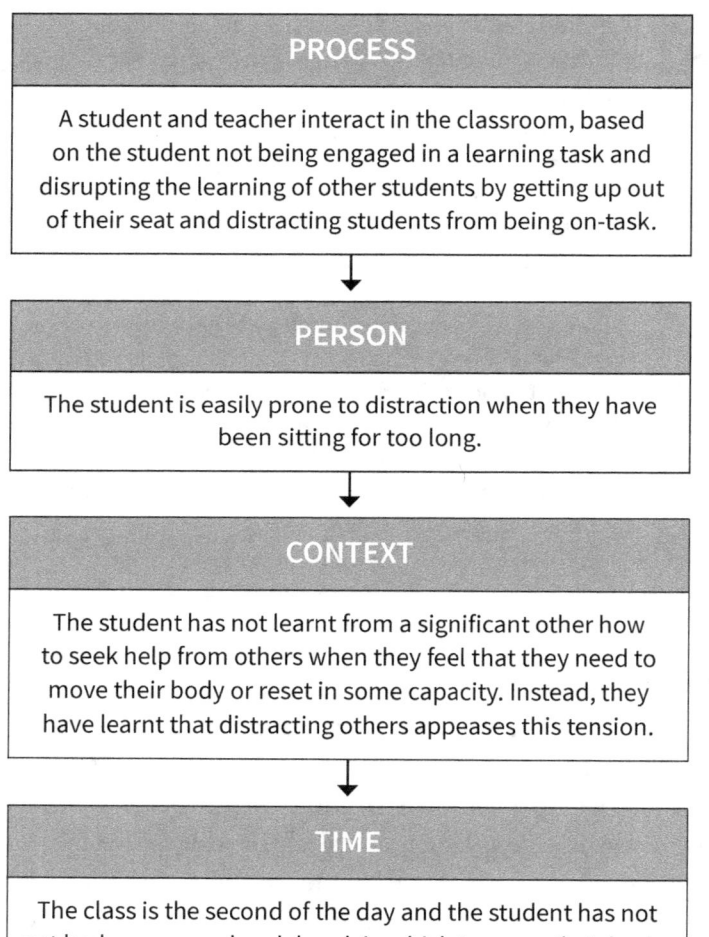

In the example, we see that the student is out of their seat and disrupting the learning of other students. By developing a thorough understanding of the student, we realise that they need movement embedded into their learning in order to stay focused, especially when they haven't had a break prior to the lesson. Concurrently, they have not had positive role modelling regarding self-regulation strategies and how to seek help when the stimulus of sitting for too long becomes challenging for them.

This example highlights the importance of developing high-growth relationships with students, and engaging in dialogue to better understand how the interaction of personal characteristics, context and time influences students' behaviours. Once you build this understanding, you can engage with certain strategies to redirect off-task behaviour (we'll look at this in Chapter 5). In the example above, this might also result in a slight change to your pedagogy to allow for some movement-based learning in the class. It may also be that you work with that student to develop strategies to build their self-regulation skills, and encourage them to communicate with you when and if they need assistance with this.

However, the buck doesn't and shouldn't stop there. While the PPCT example shows a teacher-student interaction at the level of the microsystem, there are also interactions that you can have in the student's mesosystem to enact positive behavioural change. Bronfenbrenner's work can be used as a lens to triangulate partnerships with other teachers and parents to assist with behaviour education. It is, in essence, a theory that enables us to think about how we build a geodesic dome around students that need the most support.

The remainder of this chapter looks at how the use of a functional behaviour assessment (FBA) and a behaviour support plan (BSP) can assist with this.

 ## Toolkit: Functional behaviour assessments (FBAs)

A functional behaviour assessment (FBA) is a structured and holistic approach to investigating a student's behaviour. It seeks to develop an understanding of:

- **the facade:** What behaviour is the student displaying? Are there accompanying behaviours happening at the same time?
- **the function:** What is behind the facade? What is the function of the behaviour? What is it that the student is seeking to achieve with the behaviour?
- **the context:** Where and when is the behaviour displayed? Are there common themes between the behaviour and different contexts within the school?

To inform an FBA, data is collected through formal and informal observations, surveys and interviews with teachers, the student and their parents. The data is then analysed to determine the function of the student's behaviour; that is, why does the student display that behaviour, and what happens before and after it has been displayed?

More often than not, behaviour can be associated with either accessing or avoiding certain feelings, sensations or outcomes. For example, through an FBA it might surface that the function behind a student's off-task behaviour, such as constantly calling out in class, is to access attention and credibility. The goal of the FBA would then be to develop an intervention that educates the student and reinforces more appropriate ways to access attention and credibility. One such intervention might be to enhance the student's opportunity to support the learning of others in the class.

Table 2.4 lists some common examples of what students might be accessing or avoiding when they display certain behaviours.

It is important to note, though, that a student's off-task behaviour cannot be distilled into a simple binary conclusion that a student is solely accessing or solely avoiding. It may very well be that they are accessing and avoiding at the same time, and, in many cases, they might be accessing and avoiding multiple things at once. Collecting a range of direct and indirect data assists with adding context to the analysis, as there may be certain settings or times that influence the prevalence of off-task behaviour more than others. With this knowledge, interventions are targeted so that strategies are developed to support the student with behaviour education in context.

Table 2.4: Examples of what students might be accessing and avoiding with their behaviour

Accessing	Avoiding
Attention	Attention
Recognition	Fear of failure
Praise	Physical pain
Credibility	Psychological distress
Accomplishment	Waiting
Peer acceptance	Boredom
Stimulation	Forgetting the answer
Relief of frustration	Pressure
Power	Chastisement
Self-worth	Embarrassment
Autonomy	Acceptance of the situation

The next sections explain how to conduct an FBA, with consideration firstly given to seeking consent from parents to conduct an FBA.

Seeking consent

In most cases, FBAs do not need explicit parent consent, but it is considered best practice to do so. It brings the teacher and the parent together to work constructively in the student's mesosystem. A consent form that details the process and intended outcomes of the

FBA enables parents to better understand its purpose. Some teachers might find that a student support group (SSG) meeting with parents and the principal is necessary before seeking consent to conduct an FBA.

Developing a shared understanding of the function behind the facade enables all parties to have high expectations for learning. Including parents in the FBA process enables them to build an awareness of how they, too, can support their child with their learning and behaviour outside of school. Parents can also provide invaluable insights into the specific behavioural triggers for their child, which becomes an important source of data to inform the concluding hypothesis in the FBA.

The assessment process

FBAs are conducted by a team of professionals in the field. This can include a combination of teachers, school leaders and wellbeing staff. An FBA is not considered to be a clinical process and therefore does not require specific qualifications to conduct, but general educators may need professional development in how to conduct them well. Samudre et al. (2020) conducted a systematic review of the training that teachers had received to conduct FBAs, concluding that the training was limited and many educators had simply not received any training at all. They expressed that FBA-based professional learning should be provided to all educators, as FBAs form part of school's obligation to meet the unique needs of students who engage in off-task behaviour. In support of this, others have shown that interventions stemming from FBAs are effective in reducing off-task behaviour (Jeong & Copeland, 2020; Waguespack et al., 2006).

It is, however, best to exercise discretion as to who should be involved in an FBA. For example, if the identified behaviour poses a serious risk to the health and safety of others, consideration should be given to the inclusion of regional staff, specialist support workers and medical professionals. For low-level off-task behaviours, an FBA might be conducted with only a handful of teachers alongside the principal.

Regardless of who is involved, an FBA offers a systematic way to approach behaviour education within the student's mesosystem.

The steps to conduct an FBA are as follows:

1. **Identify the problem and define the facade with others in the school:** A teacher might notice that a student's off-task behaviour appears to be more frequent and intense, and causing significant disruption to their own and/or others' learning. The student might not be responding to whole-class approaches, and, through professional conversations with other teachers, there might be some commonality across different classroom and school settings. As a team, the teachers might decide to seek approval from leadership to conduct an FBA alongside wellbeing staff in the school.

2. **Decide on how data will be collected:** The FBA team meets to decide on data that will be collected, whether that be direct (e.g. observations) and/or indirect (e.g. interviews). They decide how and when they will collect data. This process may involve deciding on observation dates, developing proformas for observation, creating surveys, developing interview questions and developing a schedule for parent contact throughout the completion of the FBA. The key here is to divide and conquer – don't do it alone! A successful FBA requires a collective team effort.

3. **Collect and analyse data to inform the FBA:** The FBA team collects and analyses data so that a thorough portrait can be painted on how antecedents, behaviour and consequences connect and correlate with one another to explain the function of the behaviour that sits behind the facade. A key thing to mention here is that an FBA is an iterative process and, as more data is collected, the FBA changes with new insights and analysis.

4. **Develop a concluding hypothesis:** The FBA team develops a concluding hypothesis for why the student is demonstrating the behaviour and what they might be accessing or avoiding in a certain context. This information is relayed to the parent and

the student in and through the development of a BSP, which is described later in this chapter.

A core component of an FBA is interviewing parents, teachers and the student themselves. These interviews might be conducted in person, where one member of the FBA team acts as the interviewer. If time and resources do not allow for this, the questions might be handed to the interviewee in hard copy. The advantage of in-person interviewing is that the interviewer can ask clarifying questions and build upon the answers provided by the interviewee. The advantage of a hard copy question sheet is that the interviewee has more time to think about and construct their answers, and this might be beneficial for students who need more time to think deeply about their behaviour. A hard copy question sheet might also better allow younger students to engage in dialogue with their parents about their behaviour.

The FBA team may even decide to do a mixture of both approaches, and this will depend upon the school's context. While the FBA questions should be tailored to the specific context of the student and the school, Table 2.5 details some sample questions that can be considered when creating interview questions for teachers, the student and parents.

Observations, too, are important because they support and triangulate the findings of the FBA interviews. A teacher might enlist the help of a colleague to observe one of their classes and make professional notes on the antecedents to the identified behaviour. This can relate to specific areas of practice, such as what happens when the student is asked to do a particular task; or it can relate to the student's behaviour when the teacher attempts to address and redirect the identified behaviour. A good way to make these observational notes is through the 'Before, When, Then' observation template, which considers the setting, the antecedent, the behaviour and the consequence of the behaviour displayed (the ABC observational method). An example of how this template might be filled in is provided in Table 2.6.

Table 2.5: Sample questions to ask in an FBA interview

Teacher	Student	Parents
What are the student's strengths, skills and interests?	What are your strengths, skills and interests are?	What are your child's strengths, skills and interests?
What does the student find challenging in the classroom?	What do you find challenging when you are in the classroom?	What does your child find most difficult regarding their learning?
What type of activities does the student engage with the most?	What activities do you like the most in school and why?	What activities does your child engage well with outside of school?
What type of activities does the student engage with the least?	What activities do you like the least in school and why?	How does your child respond to positive reinforcement at home?
What is the description of the behaviour that is interfering with learning?	What behaviours do you think negatively influence your learning? Why?	What do you believe the triggers are for the identified behaviour?
What is the frequency, duration and intensity of the behaviour?	How often do you display these behaviours?	What do you believe the intended outcomes of the identified behaviour are?
What are the precursor actions that occur prior to the behaviour being displayed?	Why do you think you display these behaviours?	What supports do you believe your child needs to better connect with their learning?
What are the environmental factors (time, people, space) that stimulate or suppress the behaviour?	What outcomes do you hope to achieve when you display these behaviours?	
What are the consequences of the behaviour?	Think back to the classroom. What helps you to remain focused and what stops you from being focused?	

Table 2.6: Sample 'Before, When, Then' template as part of FBA data collection

Observation conducted by: Rachael Date: 18/8/2023. Time: 9:00am. Class: 9a	
REFLECTIVE NOTES ON THE SETTING *(e.g. time, place, people, classroom layout, task)* The lesson was the first of the day and started at 9:00am. There were 26 students in the class. The set-up of the classroom was traditional rowed seating with the teacher delivering at the front of the class. Michael walked into the class five minutes late and immediately chose to sit in the back row next to Tom and Luke. Michael appeared to be quite tired and was yawning as soon as soon as he entered the classroom. When the teacher was explaining the instructions for the first task of the lesson, Michael had his head down on his desk. I wondered if he had had a good night's sleep last night and this might be something to investigate further. I have decided that I will speak to the wellbeing staff about Michael's tired demeanor at the completion of the observation.	
Observed behaviour 1 – off-task and defiant	
What happened before the observed behaviour? *Antecedent*	In the last half of the lesson, the teacher asked students to use their computers to research topics for an upcoming essay they were going to start writing. The teacher advised the class that they would have 20 minutes to research, and then the laptops would be placed away so that they could focus on completing a learning task related to drafting an essay outline. During the lesson, the teacher mainly focused on assisting the students at the front of the class and did not approach Michael's table group at the back of the class. The teacher did not interact with Michael in the lesson until the experienced conflict.

When statement(s) (connected to observable behaviour) *Behaviour*	When students were asked to place their computers away, I observed Michael yelling, 'There is no way that I am closing my laptop. The task is boring' very loudly. When the teacher walked over to the desk, I observed Michael telling the teacher that he was busy playing a game and that he would close the laptop when he was finished. Upon initial request by the teacher, Michael commented, 'You don't care about me anyway so go away.' When the teacher responded with a stern threat of confiscation, delivered while standing over Michael's table, I observed Michael escalating his off-task behaviour further – averting eye contact with the teacher, clenching his fists on the table and raising his voice louder with statements such as 'No', 'Go away' and 'Leave me alone, go annoy someone else.'
Then statement(s) *Consequence*	After the interaction at Michael's desk, the teacher walked away and assisted other students in the class. The teacher advised Michael that he would come back and confiscate the computer in five minutes, but this was not followed up and the teacher and Michael did not interact further in the lesson. Without a resolution, Michael continued playing games on his computer until the bell went. In total, Michael played games on his computer for approximately half the lesson (25 minutes). It appeared that Michael was communicating his desire to *avoid work* and *accept the situation*. The function behind the facade of the behaviour appeared to be accessing feelings of autonomy and engagement, with this function served in and through playing games on his laptop. This behaviour was reinforced as there was no further follow-up by the teacher after the initial interaction.
	Repeat for other observed behaviours

The example in Table 2.6 shows that Michael's behaviour in that moment was complex, and there is a whole range of factors that needed to be considered further; for example, wellbeing concerns, digging deeper into differentiation, classroom seating arrangements, the use of threats and the impact of them on Michael, and the relationship that Michael has with the teacher. It is for this reason that there must be multiple 'Before, When, Then' observation templates completed in order to contribute to the conducing hypothesis in an FBA. Simply conducting one observation is not enough. Multiple observations conducted across a variety of settings enables the contextual factors to be fleshed out. The observation data can then be displayed through a scatterplot diagram, enabling the teachers to paint a broad picture of the frequency and intensity of the behaviour and where and when it occurs most.

Once sufficient data has been collected, the FBA team must analyse them to find recurring themes to better understand the student's behaviour; that is, the function behind the facade. A hypothesis can then be created to explain how the interaction of context and the behaviour coagulate together. A template for this is provided in Table 2.7.

While conducting FBAs can be time-consuming, they enable interventions that can lead to significant improvements in students' behaviour. They can help you identify specific supports that students need to maintain a focus on their learning. They also allow you to tweak your instructional practices to cater for the diverse needs of the students in front of you.

An FBA is often a necessary precursor to the creation of successful BSP, which is discussed next.

Table 2.7: Concluding hypothesis template for an FBA

Environment Consider the evidence of the FBA and detail the biological, social, emotional, physical and task-related factors that increase the likelihood of the identified behaviour occurring.	
Biological	
Social and emotional	
Physical	
Task-related	

Concluding hypothesis

Consider the evidence of the FBA and detail a concluding hypothesis that explains the intended function of the behaviour behind the facade in context.

_____ *(student)* engages in _____ *(behaviour)* when _____ *(antecedent – add more if needed)* because when he/she/they does/do _____ *(consequence e.g. accessing or avoiding something)*.
This behaviour is most likely to happen at _____ *(time)*, during _____ *(setting)* and/or when _____ *(setting events e.g. task, people)*.

 ## Toolkit: Behaviour support plans (BSPs)

Once you have completed an FBA and developed a concluding hypothesis, you may also need to create a BSP. A BSP is a document that details agreed-upon protocols for addressing the off-task behaviour identified in the FBA and reinforcing positive alternatives. It is reified in the form of written document so that everyone who supports the student, those within their mesosystem, is able to take a consistent approach to behaviour education. A BSP focuses largely on prevention strategies so that a student has the opportunity to learn proactive ways of behaving in a particular setting. An effective BSP adopts an educative approach to behaviour management, allowing a student to develop skills in self-regulation, resilience, reflection and building respectful relationships, and ways to enhance their connection to the learning process.

The goal of a BSP is to ensure that all students and staff feel safe, valued and positively connected to others in the school community. Not all students will need a BSP, and this will come down to a school's approach to behaviour education. It may be that tweaking certain contextual factors based on an FBA results in a student's behaviour improving, so a BSP isn't needed. However, if after certain changes are made the behaviour doesn't improve, a BSP can provide further support to both the student and their teachers. If a school adopts a tiered approach to behaviour support, students who have been identified in the top tier as needing additional support will generally be those who require a BSP. Targeted BSPs can also be developed for students who have been diagnosed with severe behavioural disorders, or students who have been identified as needing additional wellbeing support.

Responsibility for BSPs

While FBAs can be completed by different teams, I suggest that one person is responsible for the oversight of BSPs in a school. This might be a leading teacher, an assistant principal or the student welfare coordinator. Whoever leads the BSPs will be responsible for making, monitoring and reviewing all BSPs in the school, as well as attending SSG meetings with parents, teachers and the student themselves. Having one person lead and coordinate the BSP process ensures that there is consistency across BSPs, as well as allowing staff and parents to have a unified port of call should there be any questions related to a specific BSP. If there are too many people responsible it gets rather messy and the process collapses.

The person responsible for BSPs in the school should engage in and coordinate the steps following.

Developing a BSP

There are six steps involved in developing a BSP, each of which is detailed following:

1. **Review the FBA and the concluding hypothesis:** The first step is reviewing the FBA and the concluding hypothesis to ascertain whether or not a BSP is warranted. There might be some environmental changes that can be made quite easily that will alleviate the off-task behaviour.
2. **Conduct an initial SSG meeting:** If a BSP is needed, conduct an SSG with relevant staff, parents and the student. The meeting should cover the impact of the off-task behaviour and the need for a BSP. It is important that these conversations are had in a respectful and supportive manner, and convey that the focus of the BSP is not punitive but rather educative. It is also a good idea in this initial meeting to ask the parents and student what they believe the appropriate strategies might be to address the identified behaviour.
3. **Conduct a meeting with relevant staff to write the BSP:** Once the initial SSG is completed, a meeting should be had with relevant staff to write the BSP. It is important that the BSP is written clearly and logically. There should be a focus on defining the off-task behaviour succinctly, and also naming the preventative (limit the behaviour), educative (replace the behaviour) and reactive (manage the behaviour) strategies for staff to employ. It is also important to develop a crisis management plan in the event that the reactive strategies do not work to stop the off-task behaviour.
4. **Conduct a follow-up SSG meeting:** With the BSP written, a second SSG meeting is needed to go through the document and facilitate an understanding of the next steps. It is important at this stage that the parents and the student are on the same page regarding how the off-task behaviour will be addressed.

Each page of the BSP should be worked through meticulously. The parents and student should be given the opportunity to ask clarifying questions, as well questions to establish the student's understanding. For example, what does that mean to you? What do you think that looks like? Can you tell me in your own words what that means? At the end of the meeting, the BSP should be signed and a copy provided to the parents. The meeting should be closed with an agreed-upon timeframe for review, which could be weekly, monthly or at the end of each term.

5. **Provide a copy of the BSP to all relevant staff in the school:** Distribute the BSP to all relevant staff in the school who teach the student. If this is a large number of staff, it might be beneficial to do this in a staff meeting. The key is to develop consistency of approach so that the student is able to develop skills to address the off-task behaviour. The biggest downfall of a BSP is a lack of consistency after it has been signed – for example, in one class the student is allowed to continue with the off-task behaviour, but in others they are not. The BSP coordinator might work with teachers to conduct further behaviour observations to review the frequency, intensity and locus of the student's behaviour.

6. **Review the BSP:** Review the BSP according to the agreed-upon review timeframe. If the behaviour has improved over time, the BSP might be concluded. However, if the student needs further support, a further SSG meeting might be needed to refine the BSP and change the preventative, educative or reactive strategies therein.

Key things to include in a BSP

There are several elements that should be included in all BSPs, including:

- known environmental triggers for the identified behaviour (use the FBA for this)
- how the behaviour is reinforced (use the FBA for this)
- preventative strategies to reduce triggers for the behaviour

- educative strategies to provide redirection towards more appropriate behaviour
- strategies to manage the behaviour when it is displayed, without reinforcing it
- how to positively acknowledge the student's efforts for behavioural change
- when and how the BSP will be reviewed.

Bambara et al. (2015) argued that, at the very least, there should be three things evident in every BSP: preventative strategies, teaching strategies and reinforcement strategies. For example, if we know the antecedent to the student's off-task behaviour, we are then able to prevent it, teach new strategies that are socially acceptable and render the function behind the facade of the off-task behaviour ineffective, while also reinforcing the replacement behaviour that ensues (see, for example, Barker et al. 2022; Dunlap et al. 2018).

All education departments in Australia have well-structured and succinct BSP templates that can be downloaded through their respective websites. The content of the templates varies slightly between states, but they all cover the prevent, teach and reinforce elements well.

CHAPTER SUMMARY AND REFLECTION

In this chapter I discussed the work of Urie Bronfenbrenner as a way of illustrating that successful behaviour education in schools is reliant upon many people working together to address students' off-task behaviours. I touched on the importance of undertaking an FBA to understand the reasoning behind off-task behaviour. Last, I considered how BSPs can be used in schools to develop preventative, educative and reactive strategies that address the identified behaviour.

Take a moment now to reflect on your learning and understanding using the *compass points* thinking tool, which is best used in dialogue with a mentor or critical friend. It will help you make connections, identify key ideas and consider the application of your learning.

- **N = Need to know:** What else do you need to know after reading this chapter? What additional information will you seek?
- **E = Employ:** What is something that you will employ in your own practice immediately or in the future?
- **S = Suggestion:** What suggestions could you make to the leadership of your school to ensure consistency of approach with FBAs and BSPs?
- **W = Wonder:** What are you wondering about after reading this chapter? Do your thoughts relate to one student in particular or a whole class?

CHAPTER 3

BECOMING A TRAUMA-INFORMED PRACTITIONER

'The children who need love the most will always ask for it in the most unloving ways.' – Russell Barkley

In *The Jungle Book*, English novelist Rudyard Kipling wrote that the strength of the pack is the wolf, and the strength of the wolf is the pack. The previous two chapters have focused much on the central tenet of this quote, demonstrating the need to work with and alongside others, including other teachers and students themselves, to ensure that behaviour education in schools is enacted in a positive, constructive and supportive way. However, much can also be said about the fact that the wolf, or wolves, in our packs may have experienced, or are continuing to experience, acute or chronic traumatic stress in their lives. As mentioned in Chapter 2, as teachers you may never truly know what is occurring in a student's microsystem or mesosystem. There might be much trauma occurring for a student, and their way of coping is illuminated in off-task behaviours in the classroom.

Often, trauma-affected students depend on us as knowledgeable, understanding and caring adults to provide them with a sense of stability and safety in their environment. For many students, school is the only place where they can gain a sense of stability and safety. It is for this reason that it would be remiss of me to not close out Part I of this book on creating a geodesic dome around students with a chapter on becoming a trauma-informed practitioner. The purpose of this chapter is to emphasise that becoming trauma-informed is essential to the successful adoption of a whole-school approach to behaviour education in schools. This is especially important when considering the creation and maintenance of FBAs and BSPs (Chapter 2) and when enacting a staged response to correcting students' off-task behaviour (Chapter 5).

The chapter starts by defining a traumatic event, childhood traumatic stress and the impact of this on student outcomes – notably the ability of trauma-affected students to self-regulate cognitively, emotionally and behaviorally. Next, we'll consider the polyvagal perspective, as this helps cement the need to build safe and secure classroom environments. I'll use a case study to explore the trauma-informed positive education (TIPE) framework and the effect it has on student outcomes. The chapter concludes with information on how to create your own sensory box for students to assist them to de-escalate from the stress response.

Chapter learning intentions

By the end of this chapter, you will be able to:

- understand what a traumatic event is and what childhood traumatic stress is
- understand the polyvagal perspective and how it relates to the stress response
- enact the TIPE framework in their own practice
- create their own sensory box to assist students to de-escalate from the stress response.

Defining a traumatic event

It is important to first provide clarity around the definition of a traumatic event and, subsequently, both the acute and chronic stress that can ensue for a child. In doing so, I aim to provide a common language around trauma so that the pedagogical strategies explained later in the chapter connect well to this first section on creating a geodesic dome around students.

Based on the definition communicated by the National Child Traumatic Stress Network (NCTSN, 2023), a traumatic event is a 'frightening, dangerous, or violent event that poses a threat to a child's life or bodily integrity'. This, too, can be extended to witnessing an event that threatens the life or physical security of a loved one or friend. The evolving definition of trauma must also acknowledge the collective, historical and intergenerational trauma of colonised Indigenous communities, particularly Aboriginal communities in Australia (Menzies, 2019).

NCTSN (2023) and others (Harden et al., 2019; Menzies, 2019) have demonstrated that a range of events can be traumatic for children, such as, but not limited to, the following:

- physical, sexual, or psychological abuse and neglect (including bullying and trafficking)
- natural and technological disasters
- family or community violence
- terrorism, mass violence and school shootings
- discrimination, prejudice and racism
- sudden or violent loss of a loved one
- substance use disorder (personal or familial)
- traumatic separation (including as part of an immigration journey, parental divorce or incarceration)
- refugee and war experiences (including torture)
- serious accidents or life-threatening illness (including ongoing medical events)
- poverty-related factors that compromise safety and security through a lack of resources to fulfill basic needs such as satisfying hunger
- historical trauma, post-colonial trauma and intergenerational trauma.

NCTSN (2023) further delineates between three types of trauma events: acute (single event), chronic (recurring events) and complex (multiple traumatic events, often invasive). Traumatic experiences can elucidate reactions, emotions and feelings that are felt at the time of the trauma(s) experienced and for long periods of time after them. NCTSN (2023) explained that traumatic reactions can include a variety of responses, such as:

- intense and ongoing emotional upset
- depressive symptoms or anxiety
- behavioural changes
- difficulties with self-regulation
- problems relating to others or forming attachments
- regression or loss of previously acquired skills
- attention and academic difficulties
- nightmares, difficulty sleeping and eating
- physical symptoms, such as aches and pains
- older children may use drugs or alcohol, behave in risky ways or engage in unhealthy sexual activity.

Child traumatic stress and its impact on student outcomes

Children who have experienced one or more traumatic events may show signs of child traumatic stress. These children 'develop reactions that persist and affect their daily lives after the events have ended' (NCTSN, 2023). For children who suffer from child traumatic stress, the symptoms described above interfere with their ability to function and interact with others in meaningful and positive ways, especially in social settings such as schools. This, in turn, affects their learning outcomes. In their review of the Berry Street Education Model (BSEM) as a whole-school approach to student engagement and wellbeing, Stokes et al. (2019) argued that it is not uncommon for students within mainstream schools, particularly those within socioeconomically disadvantaged areas, to have experienced trauma. This can lead to them displaying challenging behaviours that can disrupt not only their learning, but the learning of other students, too.

Similarly, Harden et al. (2019) showed that trauma affects children's outcomes across ages and all domains of health and functioning, such as:

- neurobiological changes that impact a child's mental and physical health
- affects on the brain regions responsible for higher-order thinking (e.g. executive functioning, memory, learning processes, language)
- lower ability to regulate emotionally and behaviourally.

Of particular interest to this book on behaviour education is the impact of child traumatic stress on a child's ability to self-regulate cognitively, emotionally and behaviourally. Panlilio et al. (2019) defined self-regulation as the ability to 'initiate control processes such as shifting attention, effortful control, managing emotions, setting goals, monitoring one's own behaviours, and engaging positively with others'. The authors argued that child traumatic stress is disruptive to a child's self-regulation processes, and, as a result, their academic and wellbeing outcomes can be severely impacted. This claim is captured in Figure 3.1, overleaf.

An inability to self-regulate may mean that a student displays certain behaviour as a way to avoid events or situations that are similar to, or generate the same thoughts and feelings as, the trauma(s) that have been experienced. A good way to think about this is through the central underpinnings of cognitive behavioural therapy (CBT). Following its inception in the 1960s by American psychologist Aaron Beck, CBT has grown to be one of the most widely used methods to understand and change emotional processes. Most would have heard of CBT as an effective treatment approach for a range of mental and emotional health issues, including anxiety and depression. However, it is also a good way to think about how and why we behave in the ways that we do.

Figure 3.1: The impact of trauma on students' self-regulation skills and outcomes

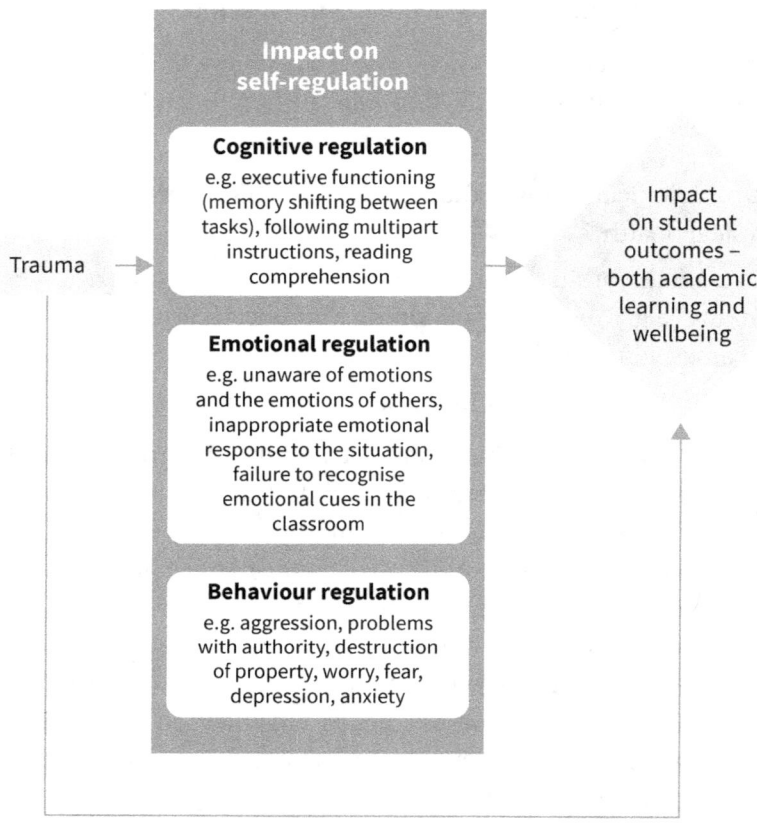

ADAPTED FROM PANLILIO ET AL. (2019).

One of the key elements of CBT is the cognitive triangle, which demonstrates the interconnected nature of how our thoughts influence our feelings and, in turn, our behaviour. Below is an explanation of the three elements of CBT:

1. **Thoughts:** how we make sense of a situation.
2. **Feelings:** feelings do not relate to our emotions, rather the physiological changes that occur in our bodies as a result of emotion.

3. **Behaviour:** the things that we do and, concomitantly, the things that we choose not to do.

The main tenet of CBT is that the combination of our thoughts, feelings and behaviours affect our quality of life. Importantly, in the context of this book, they affect how a student engages with their learning and behaves in class. We can add to the cognitive triangle an additional layer of childhood trauma, which has been shown to dramatically influence how a child views and feels about the world and responds to situations (Harden et al., 2019; NCTSN, 2023). The combination of the cognitive triangle and trauma can be best illustrated through the metaphor of an iceberg, as pictured in Figure 3.2. The behaviour that we see on the surface may have a deeper meaning, so it is important for us to become trauma-aware practitioners to support students to self-regulate – that is, to understand their thoughts, feelings and behaviour and provide them with de-escalation strategies and support.

Figure 3.2: The trauma iceberg

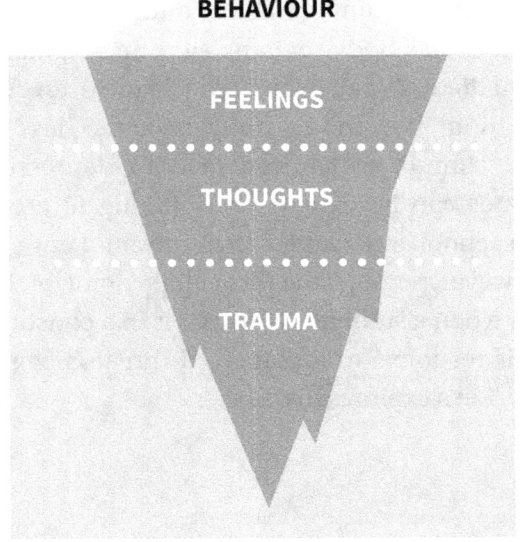

For example, a student who has witnessed domestic violence may storm out of a classroom to avoid a heightened argument with the teacher, as this may elucidate similar feelings to what they experienced during the traumatic events – for example, a loss of power, feeling scared and threatened and so on. Alternatively, some students may display behaviours that show they are accessing certain feelings, such as a sense of safety, and subsequently falling asleep in class because it is the one place they feel safe to do so. We would do well to engage in dialogue with the students in these examples about how their thoughts influence their feelings and behaviours in these situations, and co-design strategies that enhance their connectedness to learning in our classrooms.

Let's now consider a neurobiological perspective as a way to further explain why this is the case. Children who have experienced, or are experiencing, childhood traumatic stress are more prone to a dysfunctional stress responses in the brain and body. Conroy and Perryman (2022) explained that 'during a stress response, the body releases a flood of hormones to promote adaptation in response to stress, which is primarily facilitated by the hypothalamic-pituitary-adrenal (HPA) axis'. Childhood traumatic stress is strongly associated with dysfunction in the HPA axis, which leads to repeated and prolonged periods of upregulation and/or downregulation. In upregulation, a child's body remains alert and vigilant despite their being no immediate threat, which can lead to anxiety symptoms. In downregulation, the child's body becomes less responsive to environmental stimuli, which can lead to depressive symptoms. Both these states can be extremely inhibiting to a child's learning experiences in school, and can result in the child engaging in off-task behaviour. However, perhaps the most challenging of these two states for a teacher is when a student's HPE axis is in a constant upregulated state, and their response to a perceived threat is aggressive and/or argumentative. Let's explore this further.

The relationship between childhood traumatic stress, the stress response and behaviour

During the stress response, the body prioritises blood and energy flow to maximise physical agility (the flight or fight response), which leads to a shortage within the brain and an ability to cognitively rationalise ensuing decisions and actions. Childhood traumatic stress negatively impacts the areas of the brain that are responsible for emotional regulation, such as the hippocampus, amygdala and corpus collosum (Conroy & Perryman, 2022; Hart & Rubia, 2012; Teicher et al., 2002). The development of these regulatory structures in the brain are stunted as a result of childhood traumatic stress, which means that the child is more sensitive and reactive to potential threats. This leaves them in a constant state of feeling heightened and is strongly linked to behavioural outbursts and mood swings (Horn et al., 2017).

We have all been there before. You are in the middle of teaching a class and you ask a student to do, or stop doing, something and then all of a sudden the conversation seemingly descends into chaos. You might feel that the student has reacted in a way that is not in line with how the request was delivered, but in their mind, the request has been perceived as an immediate threat to their safety or welfare. It may have been a simple redirect to ask the student to please stop talking while someone else was talking, and then the next moment the chair is flipped, they have yelled every expletive under the sun, and may have even stormed out of the room. Or it may be you approach a student for a one-on-one conversation and the way the conversation begins immediately triggers the student into a heightened state where they enter fight or flight mode and become defensive, argumentative and defiant.

If you are nodding right now as you read this, just know that you are not alone – the teachers I work with often describe situations such as this as the hardest part of being an educator. I want you to know that the student in this situation needs you more than you know. It is an opportunity to be that person of stability for them, to show them that you care for them and have high expectations for their wellbeing and their learning. Remember: co-regulation breeds self-regulation.

Before I detail some trauma-informed practices that you can employ as part of your own behaviour education approach, I first want to discuss the polyvagal perspective as this helps to frame why it is important to build a culture of safety and support in our classrooms. Safe and supportive classrooms help students who have experienced, or are experiencing, childhood traumatic stress to build emotional regulation skills.

The polyvagal perspective

Stephen Porges, Professor of Psychiatry at the University of North Carolina, is credited with introducing polyvagal theory in 1995. The theory is largely centred around the vagus nerve, which is the main nerve that facilitates the body's regulatory capacities such as breathing, digestion and heart rate. The vagus nerve is part of the parasympathetic nervous system, which calms our bodies after we experience the stress response. To initiate this process, the vagus nerve sends a signal from our brains to other parts of our bodies to initiate the exit from the fight or flight response. However, childhood traumatic stress significantly influences the effect of this. Porges' (1995, 2011) theory demonstrates how the three branches of the vagus nerve influence the body's response to threat and danger (Table 3.1).

Porges (1995, 2011) explained that the dorsal vagal complex, the most primitive branch, is responsible for the freeze response, which is activated when a life-threatening situation is perceived. The consequence of this is conservation of metabolic resources as the individual shuts down in terror, becoming unable to move or connect with themselves and/or others. The sympathetic nervous system mobilises the body to fight or flee in response to danger, resulting in an increase in blood pressure, heart rate and adrenaline and a decrease in rational ability. This state of hyperarousal is focused mostly on preserving life. Last, the ventral vagal complex is activated when an individual feels a sense of safety and connectedness with their environment. This has a soothing effect on the defensive response of the sympathetic nervous system.

Table 3.1: The three branches of polyvagal theory

Action	Sense	Feeling	Bodily response
1. Parasympathetic nervous system (dorsal vagal complex)			
Freeze	Threat to life (hypoarousal)	Depression, helplessness, shame, numbness, dissociation	Increase: pain threshold, conservation of metabolic resources. Decrease: heart rate, blood pressure, temperature, social behaviour
2. Sympathetic nervous system			
Fight/flight	Danger (hyperarousal)	Rage, anger, irritation, panic, fear, anxiety	Increase: blood pressure, heart rate, adrenaline, defensive response. Decrease: fuel storage, digestion, rational ability
3. Parasympathetic nervous system (ventral vagal complex)			
Social engagement	Safety	Calm, settled, grounded, compassionate, mindful	Increase: digestion, ability to relate and connect, circulation, oxytocin. Decrease: defensive responses

ADAPTED FROM PORGES (1995, 2011).

Trauma increases the prevalence of a child's sympathetic nervous system being activated, increasing the likelihood of them displaying fear, anxiety and rage in the face of a perceived threat. Porges (1995, 2011) believed that the higher incidence of an individual's sympathetic nervous system being activated is due to a lack of soothing from the social engagement system.

Herein lies the most important message of this chapter: trauma influences how children's bodies and minds are programmed to deal with stress (real or perceived, it doesn't matter) and it is up to us as educators to help them feel more calm, settled and mindful. To do so, we must create safe and secure learning environments so that all students feel connected to their learning and can achieve success.

According to polyvagal theory (Porges, 1995, 2011), by stimulating the ventral vagal complex of individuals who have experienced trauma we can assist them in becoming less prone to states of hyperarousal. In schools, we can do this through the development of high-growth relationships with students (Chapter 1) and the provision of predictable routines, structures and classroom expectations (Chapter 4).

There has also been research on trauma-informed pedagogical strategies that can assist further. For example, the seminal work of Helen Stokes, Tom Brunzell and Lea Waters (Brunzell et al., 2016, 2019; Stokes & Brunzell, 2020) on trauma-informed positive education (TIPE) has been used by Berry Street, the largest independent child welfare organisation in Victoria, Australia, to inform the development of its trauma-informed education model. We'll look at the research on TIPE now.

Toolkit: Research on trauma-informed positive education (TIPE)

According to Stokes et al. (2019), existing trauma-informed pedagogical models have usually taken a two-tiered approach, which they argue is grounded in a deficit perspective. The first tier of these models focuses on repairing the student (e.g. improving self-regulation), and then adjusting pedagogical approaches to the developmental or learning struggles of the student. Stokes and Brunzell (2020) added that previous research has focused mostly on two siloed practice areas: *healing* through trauma-informed pedagogies and *growth* through wellbeing strategies (positive education). The latter of these two areas often includes topics such as mindfulness, character strengths, positive emotions, resilience, hope and developing a growth mindset (Brunzell et al., 2019).

In contrast, the TIPE framework includes both of these areas and adopts a strengths-based perspective, proposing three tiers of learning needed for trauma-affected students (Figure 3.3).

Figure 3.3: The trauma-informed positive education (TIPE) framework

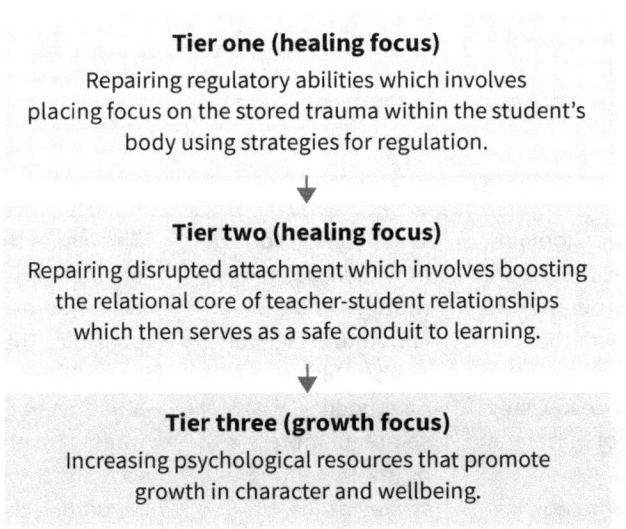

ADAPTED FROM BRUNZELL ET AL. (2016).

Brunzell et al. (2016) argued that concepts drawn from research on positive education carry important possibilities for the growth and wellbeing of students who have been affected by trauma. However, to achieve many of these outcomes, students must be 'developmentally prepared in domains such as regulatory capacities and relational abilities – domains that research shows have been compromised in trauma-affected students due to the brain-based effects of trauma'. Stokes and Brunzell (2020) added that the impetus for creating the TIPE framework was due to them witnessing too many teachers giving up on teaching wellbeing strategies to trauma-affected students, notably because the students had an overwhelming amount of regulatory and relational needs in the classroom. Thus, it is important to attend to the first two tiers before the positive education strategies taught in tier three can be absorbed by students.

The TIPE framework bridges the research between traumatology and positive education, and demonstrates a synergistic relationship between healing and growth for trauma-affected students (Stokes et al., 2019). The three tiers in the framework are explored in Table 3.2.

Table 3.2: The three tiers of the TIPE framework

Description	Strategies for teachers	Aim
Tier one: Repairing regulatory abilities		
This priority domain recognises that trauma-affected students often struggle with their own escalation in the classroom, especially if they do not understand the learning task or when their needs are not being met.	Teachers can consider how their pedagogy, routines and the curriculum facilitate opportunities for students' self-regulation by implementing strategies for co-regulation, sensory integration and mindfulness.	The aim of this tier is to create classrooms where de-escalation is possible. This includes opportunities for students to engage in multi-sensory outputs to assist them in regulating their own stress response.
Tier two: Repairing disrupted attachment		
This domain sees teachers prioritise increasing relational capacity with students. This is primarily done through the creation and maintenance of high-growth relationships, as discussed in Chapter 1.	Teachers can build secure relationships with students based on unconditional positive regard. Teachers can also prime the classroom with elements of play and fun.	Trauma-affected students often come to school with histories of ruptured relationships. The aim of this tier is to create and sustain healthy relationships with students who resist relational interactions.

Description	Strategies for teachers	Aim
Tier three: Increasing psychological resources		
This domain sees elements of positive education permeating pedagogy to increase student wellbeing.	Teachers can anchor the curriculum in character strengths, consider elements of flow principals for engagement, and intentionally teach growth mindset skills for learning.	The aim of this tier is to create classroom environments where students increase psychological resources for wellbeing and personal growth.

ADAPTED FROM STOKES AND BRUNZELL (2020).

Over the last few years of researching the use of the TIPE framework in schools, Stokes, Brunzell and Waters have concluded that transforming schools from trauma-affected to trauma-aware requires a complete shift in school culture. In the case study research that these authors have conducted, they found that where TIPE pedagogy has improved student academic and wellbeing outcomes, 'there was a comprehensive re-evaluation of the practices, daily rhythms, and curriculum to ensure that the values and goals of each staff member were aligned' (Stokes & Brunzell, 2020). These authors have found that school leadership plays an important part in the success of implementing a TIPE approach in schools, as leadership teams have the ability to galvanise the entire school community towards a common vision in and through professional learning communities, which improve teachers' personal and professional capacities.

The next section summarises a case study to illustrate how the principal of a school can use TIPE to improve student outcomes.

The TIPE framework in use

Stokes and Brunzell (2019) conducted a case study of a rural primary school that was located in a socio-economically disadvantaged community in Victoria, Australia. The study explored the role of the principal in enacting the implementation of TIPE as professional development for the school's teachers. The purpose was to equip teachers with an understanding of, and an ability to meet, students' learning and wellbeing needs.

Over a 12-month timeframe, the principal organised for the teachers to be provided with a series of sequenced training sessions based on much of what has been written in this chapter, as well as the support of curriculum materials to increase their capacity to work with trauma-affected students. The principal prioritised weekly whole-staff meetings to allow teachers to model and share learning activities and approaches to behavioural support that they were finding successful in their classrooms.

The effect of the TIPE program on Grade 5 and 6 student outcomes over the 12 months was substantial. Stokes and Brunzell (2019) noted that:

- the Grade 5 students increased their reading focus in class from 36 seconds to 20 minutes
- the Grade 5 and 6 reading groups reported an increase of four to five times the standard learning growth in one year (effect size of 2.09 and 1.18 respectively)
- the students' attitude to school survey data showed an increase in students feeling connected to the school and confidence with their learning
- the suspension rate across the 12-month period fell from 57 students to seven students.

The results from this study show the power of teachers building an understanding of the three tiers and providing students with opportunities for both co-regulations and self-regulation in the classroom. The results also demonstrate the power of building high-growth relationships with students in concert with context.

Toolkit: Repairing regulatory abilities

In the first domain of the TIPE framework there is an emphasis on repairing trauma-affected students' regulatory ability. As Brunzell et al. (2016) stated, 'this domain addresses the specific effects of trauma on the body and the neurosequential principals which guide the developmental understandings of individual student needs'. Often, trauma-affected students cannot easily access the cognitive flexibility that is needed to engage in social and emotional learning programs. There are times when in order trauma-affected students will need sensory experiences to de-escalate from the stress response. For example, when asked to reflect on how they feel, these students may not have the language, readiness or ability to easily articulate to others the connection between their emotional state, how their body feels and their behaviour. However, Stokes and Brunzell (2016) explained that trauma-affected students can be taught to improve their skills with this by recognising somatosensory cues in their body (e.g. pressure, temperature, force, tension) and connecting these cues to different emotional states, with support and guidance.

Professor Marc Bracket published an excellent book in 2019, *Permission to Feel*, which can help you with this. It is, without a doubt, one of the best books I have read, and I consider it essential reading for educators and parents. A key part of the book is developing a more thorough understanding of our emotions. For example, we are quick to label ourselves as angry when we associate that emotion with feelings of tenseness in our body. However, when we are in the red zone of Brackett's (2019) Mood Meter, which is a quadrant based on the circumplex model of affect and defines emotions across the two dimensions of pleasantness and energy, we might actually be feeling anxiety, rage, frustration or fear rather than anger. (Visit https://marcbrackett.com/about/mood-meter-app to view the Mood Meter.) Without a proper awareness of how we are feeling in the moment we are unable to *label* our current emotional state (we don't know what we don't know!) and then express how we are feeling, which are both key to regulating our emotional state. Developing an understanding of the complexity and nuances of the many different emotions we feel as humans helps us to better support trauma-affected students, and indeed all students, too.

In the book, Brackett (2019) details the RULER approach, an evidenced-based approach to social and emotional learning developed at the

Yale Center for Emotional Intelligence, which can be used alongside the Mood Meter. I would not do the RULER approach justice by attempting to summarise the complexity of the research behind it in one paragraph, so I implore you to visit the RULER website (www.rulerapproach.org) to have a look at all the resources that speak to its development, the associated professional learning and how to enact the approach in schools. An overview of the different components of the RULER approach, as well as some associated questions to ask students, is detailed in Table 3.3.

Table 3.3: The RULER approach

R	Recognising emotions	Where are you on the mood meter? Pleasant on the x-axis and energy on the y-axis.
U	Understanding the causes and consequences of emotions	What caused you to feel this way?
L	Labelling emotions and building a nuanced vocabulary	What word best describes how you are feeling? Why?
E	Expressing emotions in context	How are you showing that feeling at the moment? Internally and externally.
R	Regulating emotions through co-regulation and self-regulation strategies	What strategy will you use to feel more, less or the same as what you are feeling?

ADAPTED FROM BRACKETT (2019).

In my student management roles, I often had trauma-affected students come to my office in an incredibly heightened state. They had either been removed from the class by the teacher after an altercation, or they had self-exited and made their way to see me in my office. I didn't mind the latter as it meant they weren't walking around the school grounds in fits of rage, and it had indicated that I had managed to build trusting, secure relationships with the most challenging students where they sought me out to help them co-regulate. Such is the power of focusing on building high-growth relationships with all students who cross your path, regardless of whether or not you are in a leadership role in a school.

Often, when these students came to me, I'd first focus on doing a breathing technique together as an immediate way to decrease heart rate, blood pressure and a racing mind. Whenever my door flung open and a student stood there, yelling every expletive under the sun trying to explain what had just happened, I would approach the student calmly and with unconditional positive regard. I would ask the student to come and take a seat in the corner of the office on the comfy couches. Together, we would do an activity such as box breathing, which is a simple yet effective technique. It involves breathing in for four seconds, holding for four seconds, breathing out for four seconds, holding for four seconds, and then repeating for four cycles. Figure 3.4 provides a visual summary of how to do the box breathing activity.

Figure 3.4: Box breathing activity

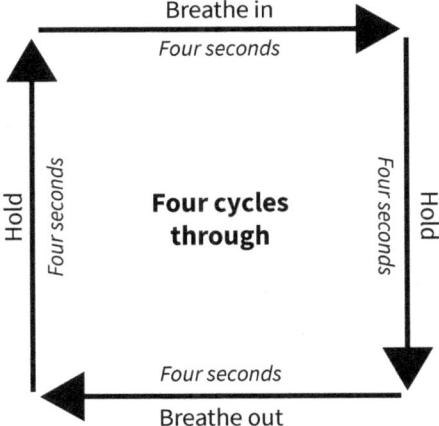

Once the student had de-escalated enough to communicate with me in more words than just expletives, I would next focus on providing them with a sensory experience and talk to them about how they were feeling using the Mood Meter and the RULER approach (Brackett, 2019). I experienced much success with this approach and found it to be a great way to better understand the student and the situation that had just occurred in the classroom.

Over the years I collected a whole range of items that were palpable or moveable and I stored them in a sensory box under my desk. I used the items in the box to initiate initial conversations with students. We'd sit on the couch together and both choose an item, and we'd first discuss the properties of the item. I'd ask questions of the student: 'What have you got? Why did you choose that? How does it feel? What can you do with it?' I found this split-second shift in focus to work wonders for resetting a student, and it was a great primer before we chatted about how they were feeling and got to the nuts and bolts of the actual incident.

When we did move on to discussing the issue at hand, we would still be using the sensory items. I would ask questions to ascertain the situation, the student's feelings in the moment, the behaviour that ensued and the consequence of that behaviour. I'd almost always follow that exact same protocol, and I would ensure that I listened intently to the student so that I could get a complete narrative of what had happened in their eyes. Most of the time, after these conversations, we would then move on to have a re-entry conversation (Chapter 5) or a restorative justice conversation together with the teacher at the end of the day (Chapter 6).

The sensory box was pivotal to the successful co-regulation with students, and it is a good example of enacting a strategy from the first tier in the TIPE framework – providing the students an opportunity to de-escalate through sensorimotor experiences. Figure 3.5 is a photo of the some of the items from one of my original sensory boxes.

The items in this photo are as follows:

1. playdough
2. physio ball
3. hacky sack
4. bounce goo
5. metal puzzle
6. rubber push circles

7. fidget box
8. leather buckle
9. snake puzzle
10. plastic spinner
11. wooden spinner.

Figure 3.5: An example sensory box for teachers

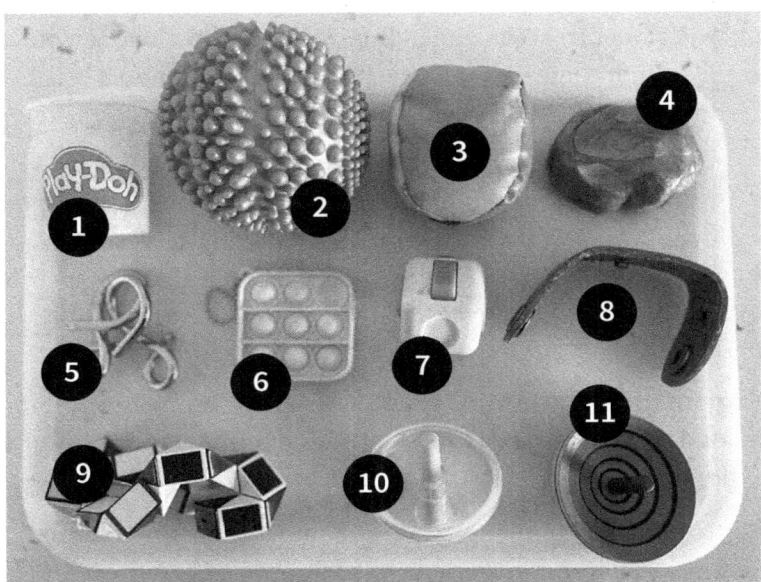

As a key recommendation from this chapter, I implore you to make your own sensory box. You can get really creative with what you include in your own sensory box, but I will state the obvious here – no sharp objects and nothing that can be used to endanger the health or wellbeing of the student, yourself or others in the school.

CHAPTER SUMMARY AND REFLECTION

In this chapter I discussed how trauma and traumatic childhood stress affects a student's learning and wellbeing outcomes. I presented the polyvagal perspective and the TIPE framework to prompt thinking about how best to implement trauma-informed pedagogy into our classrooms. In essence, trauma-informed pedagogy is the glue that holds our geodesic dome together. It is a perspective that sees off-task behaviours as an opportunity to educate rather than something to punish. There is no doubt that it is very challenging for teachers to attend to the behaviours of students who have experienced trauma, but it's important to keep in mind that some of these students may never have had a responsible adult role-model expected ways of behaving. The central message in this chapter is that teachers have the opportunity help trauma-affected students *heal* and *grow* by building safe and supportive classrooms, which underpins a successful behaviour education approach in schools.

Take a moment now to reflect on your learning and understanding through the *step in, step out, step back* thinking tool, which is best used in dialogue with a mentor or critical friend. It helps you to make connections, identify key ideas and consider the application of your learning.

- **Step in:** After reading this chapter, what are your assumptions related to what a trauma-affected student might feel, believe and experience in your classroom? Your school?

- **Step out:** Have a conversation with another teacher about the feelings, beliefs and experiences of trauma-affected students in your school. You might do this through conversation with a critical friend or mentor. What are the commonalities? What are the differences? What did you find most interesting about this conversation?

- **Step back:** Reflect upon your initial assumptions and contrast these with the conversation you had with another teacher. What did you notice about your perspective after this conversation? What did you learn? What questions do you have? What professional learning might you seek to better understand how to support trauma-affected students in your school?

PART II

WALKING THE WIRE

'It's very easy to walk on a wire when you spend your whole life practicing for it.' – Philippe Petit

During the early hours of 7 August 1974, French street performer, Philippe Petit, stepped onto the roof of the south tower of the World Trade Center in New York City. He positioned himself over 400 metres in the air and began the 40-metre tightrope walk between the south and north towers. He did this with no safety net. The story behind *le coup* is just as remarkable as the actual feat of walking between the two buildings. The night before the walk saw Petit and some accomplices, split into two teams, make their way into the towers. One of the team members shot an arrow across the gap between the towers, which was then used as a guide to string the support wire across the towers.

During his performance, Petit spent 50 minutes out there on the wire, completing eight trips across the gap and even stopping at one point to lie down on the wire – which, I must add, was only 2.5 centimetres thick. Once Petit dismounted from the wire he was charged by police for trespassing and disorderly conduct, but these charges were dropped shortly after in exchange for him performing for the public in Central Park.

When he reflected upon *le coup*, Petit was often asked if what he was doing was an artistic statement (a few people even asked if he was insane, which psychological assessments proved he was not). Petit insisted that his famous walk between the twin towers was not an artistic statement and was instead reflective of his natural disposition in life: 'I see three oranges, and I have to juggle. I see two towers, and I have to walk.' Essentially, Petit saw the walk as a celebration of passion.

Years later, Petit was quoted as saying, 'I was not gambling my life. I was doing something much more beautiful. I was carrying my life across the wire.' It was clear that Petit loved the challenge of performing and he was well-known for his preparedness. In his words: 'I am a madman of details. If you see how carefully I prepare for any kind of walk, legal or illegal, small or big, you will see that, actually, I narrow the unknown to virtually nothing. And that is when I am ready to walk on the wire.'

When I reflected on how to introduce the second part of this book I could think of no better way than with the story of Phillippe Petit. Now, in no way am I suggesting that you all now need to go and start tightrope walking. Please do not do this. Rather, I hope you might see Petit's story as a metaphor for your passion for teaching and, in the context of this book, walking the wire of behaviour education.

Petit was a master planner. Before each walk he inspected both anchor points intently before crossing, ensuring that these anchor points were secure enough to allow him to conduct the walk itself. While out on the wire, he adjusted his movements depending upon the sway of the rope and force of the wind. I contend that the practicality of behaviour education can be thought of in much the same way. At the start of our journey, we have our first anchor point which I refer to as preventative practice strategies. At the other end of the rope, we have a second anchor point in restorative justice practices. Ensuring that these anchor points are in place allow us to securely walk the wire of behaviour education, adjusting our in-the-moment practices to suit the context of our individual classes.

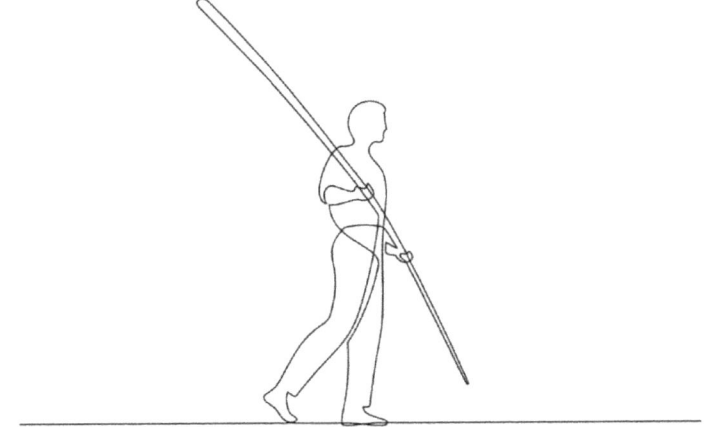

Part II of this book is divided into three chapters focused on behaviour education strategies. Chapter 4 discusses preventative practice strategies, Chapter 5 discusses in-the-moment corrective strategies, and Chapter 6 explores the concept of restorative justice and how to conduct restorative justice conference conversations with students. When considered together, these three chapters can help to build your confidence to walk the wire of behaviour education in your classroom.

CHAPTER 4

PREVENTATIVE PRACTICE STRATEGIES

'Begin with the end in mind.' – Stephen Covey

It is now time to turn our attention towards practices that we can employ to establish and maintain positive classrooms. First and foremost, we must shift our focus towards prevention over management. The major challenge for teachers is not so much the management of off-task behaviour, but knowing what to do so that off-task behaviour is less likely to occur in the first place. US politician and inventor Benjamin Franklin once said, 'An ounce of prevention is worth a pound of cure' – and this is no more pertinent than when it comes to adopting a behaviour education approach in schools. When we focus on building high-growth relationships with students and enacting preventative practice strategies in our classrooms, we model our role as classroom leaders. Too often we turn our attention to the behaviours that we don't want to see, and we miss golden opportunities to acknowledge students who display, or are working towards displaying, the expected behaviours in our classrooms. These moments are opportunities to harness. In this chapter, I implore you to adopt the core strategies that I write about as simple, yet effective, ways that you can prevent off-task behaviour from occurring in the first instance.

The chapter starts with reference to the work of Sutherland et al. (2019) and their study of 24 practice elements that teachers use to positively influence students' behavioural development. Next, I'll discuss seven of these practice elements to provide you with some strategies that you can employ when seeking to lead positive classrooms. The chapter concludes with a reflection activity on how you might use these strategies tomorrow, next week and in the future.

Chapter learning intentions

By the end of this chapter, you will be able to:

- know the 24 practice elements for improving students' behavioural development
- enact seven preventative practice strategies as part of a behaviour education approach
- reflect on how you might enact these seven preventative practice strategies in your teaching tomorrow, next week and beyond.

Promoting students' social, emotional and behavioural learning

Sutherland et al. (2019) conducted a systematic review of evidenced-based programs and practices delivered by teachers designed to address the behavioural challenges of students identified as at risk for emotional and behavioural disorders. Across the more than 100 studies included in the review, the authors identified 24 common practices that teachers successfully used to promote students' social, emotional and behavioural development. This included 12 content-based practices and 12 delivery-based practices (Table 4.1).

There is not enough space in this chapter to fully explore each of the 24 items in detail, but all the elements fit under the umbrella of behaviour education. Indeed, many of the elements have already been spoken about in this book as they relate to building referent power with students through high-growth relationships. Many more of the practices are spoken about in the chapters that follow this one. The seven elements highlighted in Table 4.1 are explicitly discussed in this chapter as four preventative practice strategies that teachers can employ as part of their own behaviour education practice. However, there is quite a large crossover with these elements and so the strategies that follow in this chapter can just as easily be attributed to some of the other elements, too.

Table 4.1: The 24 practices for improving students' learning outcomes

Content-based practices		
Helps students regulate their emotions	Helps students independently manage their social and academic behaviours	Engages constantly with parents
Provides differentiated instruction	Provides instructional feedback and discussion	Arranges for peer tutoring to occur
Helps students generate and evaluate solutions to social, behavioural and academic problems	**Reinforces positive behaviours**	**Provides routines around common tasks and transitions**
Helps students develop prosocial skills	Actively listens to students during interactions	**Promotes group responsibility for desired behaviours**
Delivery-based practices		
Actively engages in and monitors students' behaviour	Ensures behavioural momentum	Provides the students opportunities for choice in learning activities
Provides corrective feedback following the demonstration of off-task behaviour	**Models desired behavioural or academic skills to promote learning**	Actively seeks opportunities for students to respond to questions or prompts

Delivery-based practices (cont.)		
Provides behaviour-specific praise (BSP)	Engages in precorrection	Removal of reinforcements from the students in response to undesirable behaviour
Establishes behavioural expectations in the classroom	Considers primary and secondary rewards in response to desired behavioural responses	Removes students from an activity following the occurrence of misbehaviour

ADAPTED FROM SUTHERLAND ET AL. (2019).

Toolkit: Preventative practice strategies

Create a team vibe

Promotes group responsibility for desired behaviours

Reinforces positive behaviours

Models desired behavioural or academic skills to promote learning

It is no good having high expectations for students' learning if they do not know what those expectations are. Your expectations need to be clearly articulated so students can display the behaviours associated with those expectations. This is recognised as Strategy 3 in the Department of Education Victoria's *High Impact Wellbeing Strategies* (Allen et al., 2022). When articulating your expectations, you must make it clear that you hold the same expectations for each student who walks into your classroom. No-one gets a free pass. State your expectations positively, communicating exactly what the students need to do to be successful. Importantly, your communicated expectations should help students understand what they need to *do* rather than what they *shouldn't do* in the class. It is, simply, explicit instruction around the behaviours and attitudes that are expected for all students, and for yourself, as a team of collaborative learners in the classroom.

You must also make sure your expectations are expressed in a concrete rather than abstract way. For example, 'show respect' is abstract; 'when someone is talking or presenting their viewpoint we listen intently' is concrete. The number of expectations should be limited to around three to five so as to not cognitively overload the students.

Often, your expectations will be tied to the school's values. The incorporation of student voice in the descriptors for each expectation ensures that you are valuing dialogue with students as a core part of building high-growth relationships. If your school adopts a school-wide positive behaviour for learning (PBL) framework, you will see these expectations presented in the form of a behaviour matrix. The school values will be presented on the left side of the matrix; the different contexts of the school will be at the top of the matrix – classroom, yard, corridors, community, canteen area, online and so on. The middle of the matrix will be filled with concrete expectations for the school community as to how the school value is enacted in different contexts. For example, in the yard, 'we show respect taking care of the school environment and picking up after ourselves'. In the corridors, 'we show respect by entering the classroom in an orderly manner'.

In my own classrooms, I would provide students with two broad expectation themes: we are respectful, and we are organised. I would then leverage Socratic seminars to engage students in structured discussion, filling in a whole-class expectations template where explicit descriptors are extrapolated from the group. We'd discuss, critique and engage in dialogue around the expectations, and then come up with ideas as to what that looks like for both the students and the teacher. Once this was done, I'd print off a copy for each student to paste inside their books, or I'd laminate it for them to keep inside their laptop bags. This approach does take time, but I can assure you that it will pay off in the long run. Spend time early getting this right and, if you see it's worthwhile, you can revisit the same process each term so that everyone is anchored back to the expectations after the term break. Table 4.2 is a sample classroom expectation template.

Table 4.2: A whole-class expectations for learning template

Broad expectation themes	Explicit descriptors (no more than three for each)	What does successful behaviour look like for the students?	What does successful behaviour look like for the teacher?
We are respectful	We allow all voices to be heard. When someone is talking, we listen intently and don't interrupt the person speaking.	Students focus on what the person talking is saying and don't talk over them or engage in behaviour that disrupts the person talking.	The teacher allows each student the opportunity to speak during class discussions. They actively invite students to speak who haven't had the opportunity to do so.
We are organised	We devote maximum time to learning in each class. We engage in behaviour that allows for this to occur.	Students bring all required learning materials to class, and are ready to learn as soon as the lesson begins.	The teacher arrives early to the lesson to let students in so that the lesson can start on time.

Here is how you can facilitate a Socratic seminar with students around classroom expectations:

1. Arrange students into two circles of equal numbers – an inner and outer circle.
2. Ensure students all have a pen and paper so that they can take notes.
3. Pose a question around a broad expectation theme to the inner circle, such as: 'What does this expectation theme look like in practice for us as a class, which includes you as the students and me as the teacher?' The inner circle of students discusses the question. They can only address one other, not the teacher nor

the students in the outer circle. The teacher acts as a facilitator, and only speaks if the discussion needs to be redirected or prompted to spark discussion.
4. The outer circle listens to the discussion and takes notes, focusing on any points they would like to expand upon or ask a question about.
5. After a set period of time, when the points made start to repeat, or when the conversation slows, the inner circle is invited to end their discussion.
6. At the end of the discussion, the outer circle uses their notes to comment on the discussion. Members of the outer circle offer feedback or pose further questions to the inner circle.
7. Members of the inner and outer circle swap, and repeat steps two through to five. This time another expectation might be posed.
8. At the end of the discussion, the teacher and students work together to fill in the expectation template, based on the discussion, the notes from the students, and observations from the teacher.

Cement statements – celebrating good moments with the class

When things are going well in your classroom and students are engaged in on-task learning behaviours, it is a great opportunity to reinforce the positive behaviours that you are seeing. Often, we choose to sit back and relish these moments without saying anything; but it is in these moments that we should be doing the most work as teachers! We can build a lot of goodwill with students by walking around the room and cementing how much we value these 'good moments' and why. I use the term 'cement' because it is a good metaphor for what these statements achieve – they lock in and reinforce group responsibility for positive behaviours. These cement statements are directed at the whole class and related to the expectations for learning template that you have developed together. For example, you might use cement statements such as the following:

- 'I appreciate how everyone has taken initiative to start work straight away. It shows that, as a class, we are highly organised today. Thank you.'

- 'It is great to see everyone working quietly and intently focused on the task this morning in class. We agreed as a class that this fitted within our expectation of being organised and we are definitely showing that today.'
- 'I really value how we listened intently to the person speaking throughout that whole activity. It meant that everyone had a say and we showed a high level of respect towards each other and our class as a whole.'
- 'I have really valued that each and every one of you today has raised their hand during the discussion so as to not interrupt the person speaking. Thank you. We have been very respectful towards each other this lesson.'

Using cement statements such as these establishes whole-class goodwill. Doing so shows that you are focused on acknowledging positive behaviours in your classroom. It builds students' collective efficacy as they know that, together, they can build a positive classroom environment. This improves student engagement, minimises classroom disruptions and brings the focus of the lesson to learning.

Focus on what you want to see rather than what you don't

Provides behaviour-specific praise (BSP)

Reinforces positive behaviours

BSP is much the same as the cement statements I described in the previous section, but directed towards an individual student. In BSP, the teacher provides the student with a positive statement that acknowledges their on-task efforts, desired behaviours and dispositions to learning.

Teachers often use positive verbal reinforcement to encourage and motivate students. However, as Greer (2017) states, 'teachers may overly praise students or, in an attempt to spare a student's feelings, provide artificial praise when none is warranted'. Interestingly, providing an external reward such as praise to students for something that is already intrinsically motivating to them actually reduces their level of intrinsic motivation for doing that activity (Ryan & Deci, 2017).

Although research has shown that praise, when it is warranted, can increase students' intrinsic motivation to engage in desired learning behaviours (Dweck, 2006; Ryan & Deci, 2017), it needs to be targeted and directed toward students' behaviours or dispositions. American psychologist Carol Dweck emphasised this in her 2006 book, *Mindset: The New Psychology of Success*, where she stated that praise should be directed towards a student's effort instead of their intelligence. Dweck identified two mindsets – fixed and growth – both of which develop from the way that children experience praise. The fixed mindset sees intelligence as a static characteristic in an individual, but a growth mindset acknowledges that intelligence is dynamic, and individual effort is the catalyst for growth. When students are given praise for their intelligence in a fixed manner (e.g. 'You are very intelligent'), their learning is provisional because their success is attributed to a seemingly innate quality instead of the effort they put into the task itself (Greer, 2017). Rather than saying to a student, 'You are very intelligent', you might reframe the comment to, 'You displayed a lot of persistence to stick with that problem and figure it out.'

BSP is most effective when it is delivered immediately or shortly after the observable behaviour. When you deliver BSP to a student, make sure to consider their preferences for receiving feedback, whether that be in front of peers, a positive note on student management systems such as Compass, or in private after class. The procedure for delivering BSP is as follows:

1. **Scan the classroom:** During the lesson (instructional time, transitions between activities, individual work, group work), look for students engaging in desired behaviours as per the whole-class expectations template.
2. **Deliver praise:** Provide the student with BSP by using their name, then describe the behaviour that you have noticed, and then acknowledge the outcomes, results or connection to expectations.

For example, 'Jack, thanks for getting your workbook out and starting work straight away. It showed how dedicated you are to your learning in the lesson today.'

The magic ratio

Building high-growth relationships with students is premised upon you focusing on the behaviours you want to see rather than the behaviours you don't. According to relationship researcher John Gottman, the 'magic ratio' of positive to negative feedback is five to one. This means that for every one negative interaction, or, in our case, for every one comment to correct behaviour, there must be at least five positive interactions. If you have had to correct a student's behaviour, it is good to note in your memory that the next interaction with that student should entail BSP, and it will be more powerful if the BSP you provide is related to the behaviour that you have had to correct.

The five to one ratio is a great way to build referent power with students through high-growth relationships. In my own research I have found that the five to one ratio of BSP to corrective conversations dominates the lexicon in successful schools. It is engrained in practice, and it is remarkable to observe it free flowing and natural in execution.

Implement classroom systems

Provides routines around common tasks and transitions

Establishes behavioural expectations in the classroom

Students learn to demonstrate appropriate behaviours in much the same way that they learn instructional content. In the *High Impact Teaching Strategies* developed by the Department of Education Victoria (2023), 'explicit instruction' and 'worked examples' are two of the ten strategies. I contend that these strategies are also important for teaching expected behaviour in class. Using explicit teaching and worked examples (modelling) ensures that behaviour education occurs *before* behaviour management. That is, you should explicitly teach students about the behaviours associated with a given expectation, and then model the desired behaviours that are aligned with the expectation. You can also use examples of how students can meet or not meet expectations to clarify the expected behaviour. Once this is done, and everyone is on the same page with the same expectations, you have a reification point to refer to when redirecting behaviour. This is most important for routines and transitions in the classroom, which we'll discuss next.

Task analysis – think like a hip-hop dance instructor!

It is important to note that teaching a specific routine often requires you as the teacher to break the task down into meaningful chunks, and then practise those chunks individually and then together with the other chunks. And it most certainly will not be perfect first go! Think of yourself as a hip-hop dance instructor teaching a specific routine. For someone to learn the routine, you will have to break the dance down into specific movement sections that can be practised independently of each other, and then bring them together to perform the whole routine. To ensure that the hip-hop routine is learnt correctly, you will also more than likely have to practise it more than once, and embrace mistakes as part of the learning journey! Perhaps it might take a few weeks. Maybe a few months. The point here is that routines take time to embed and get right. They need to be practised and you, as the hip-hop instructor, need to break the routines down into sections and model how those sections can be performed successfully. This will often require you to undertake a task analysis; that is, what are the steps involved in this routine that need to be differentiated?

For example, a task analysis of entering the classroom at the start of a lesson might look like this:

1. Line up in two rows outside the classroom with all required learning materials.
2. Once everyone is lined up and ready, quietly walk into the classroom one person at a time.
3. Locate your allocated desk.
4. Place your learning materials on the desk.
5. Take a seat behind the desk.
6. Start the 'do now' activity that is on your table (I'll explain this later in the chapter).

When you have a routine such as this broken down into smaller steps, you can then begin the task of teaching the routine. To teach routines such as the one above, you will need to:

1. Clearly tell students what the routine is and what steps they need to do in the routine. Students need to know this information so they know how they can be successful.
2. Use visual supports to help students know what success looks like. These visual supports are more impactful if they relate to the steps in sequence with one another.
3. Demonstrate what each step looks like and ask questions of the students to develop an understanding of which steps may need more focus than others. Allow the students to ask questions, too. There may be some words that need defining or some movements that need further clarification and distinction. You may also need to model certain steps along with students more than other steps so that they can see a successful example of it in practice.
4. Practise the routine multiple times. You may need to do some steps of the routine together, and, perhaps, others might need to be practised over and over again independently of other steps.
5. Last, but not least, deliver BSP to students so that they know they are on the right track with the routine. You might have to focus on delivering lots of BSP early on, but as the routine becomes established the need for BSP may be lessened.

We cannot assume that the mere establishment of a routine means that students will understand what is expected of them. To build and embed successful routines, we must first undertake a task analysis and understand how we might break a routine down for students so that everyone in the class can experience success. We also need to model what success looks like to students and practise, practise, practise!

Some common examples where a task analysis is appropriate to embed classroom routines include:

- lining up outside the classroom before entering

- classroom entry and exit
- general movement within the classroom
- transitions between activities
- what to do at the end of an activity
- using classroom supplies
- what to do in the period of time (usually two to five minutes) before the end of the lesson.

In my own practice, I have focused intently on routines for entering the classroom. This is something that I have always aimed to educate students on because, to me, if we can get this right then we are able to maximise learning time in the lesson. As part of this, I am not averse to having students line up outside of a classroom. It has, however, taken me a long while to get comfortable with this. Originally, I had opted not to do it, and felt that it was too authoritarian. Then, after many years of teaching in small rooms with equally small corridor spaces, I realised how chaotic schools can be when there are six or seven classes all lingering outside in a common corridor waiting to enter. Inevitably I would open the door and it would be like a bull stampede over me to get into the classroom. I had to learn the hard way with this! I evolved my practice to place much emphasis on calmness and order outside of the classroom before we even entered it. It was as much a mindset as it was a process to ensure students entered the classroom in a safe and orderly manner. If we entered calmly, then I felt that was a good indication to the students of the expectation I have of them inside the classroom as learners. In the end I learnt that lining up wasn't an authoritarian approach, rather it was an authoritative approach and it was needed to establish calmness and order at the start of my lessons.

For each class, I established a routine with me standing at the door smiling and greeting the students politely and asking them to line up in a double line. I would then use the *narrative appraisal strategy*, which is a strategy that sees you focus on the global efforts first (sections, rows, groups) and then move on to local efforts (individual students) as the narrative continues. It helps to alert students to those who are displaying the expected behaviour and what we are continuing to wait for. An example of the narrative review strategy follows:

> 'It is great to see that the first two rows are lined up ready to go. Thank you Mary, Jack, Oscar, and Renee. We are still waiting for others at the back to line up. We will continue to wait.
>
> 'Matthew, I can see now that you have moved into the line, thank you. Rebecca and Lisa I can see that you have now moved into line and are quietly facing the front ready to go. Thank you to you both.
>
> 'Okay, it looks like we are all lined up and ready to enter the classroom.'

Once this was done and all students were lined up, I would get their attention using a visual or verbal prompt, such as having my hand in the air. This would signify to the students that we were all lined up and that I was requesting all eyes on me and no talking between students. Once I had everyone's focus I would offer a cement statement to the class, such as:

> 'Thank you everyone. It appears that everyone is ready to enter the classroom today and engage with the lesson. Thank you for lining up so efficiently today.'

We would then walk inside the classroom in pairs and I would say hello to each student individually. In many classes I also had a seating plan so the students knew exactly where to sit once they entered the classroom, and we had established (and practised many times) an agreed-upon way to enter the classroom and find their seats while I was at the door greeting the other students.

The above sounds great in practice, and it was, but it would be too evangelical of me to suggest that I nailed this right from the start. I did not. It took an intent focus on my behalf to ensure that entering the classroom was a routine that formed part of my high expectations for all the students I taught. Sometimes, if we did not get this right, we would not start the lesson and I would bring the students out of the classroom to try it again. This was not done as a punitive measure; it was quite the opposite. I was cognisant of the fact that some needed more practice to get this right, and I afforded particular classes more time with this than others so that everyone could experience success. I adopted a hip-hop instructor mindset to do so.

There were some classes that needed more focus on practice with lining up outside the classroom, and some that needed more assistance with establishing agreed-upon ways to enter the classroom and take their allocated seats. For some, we had to break down the routine into even smaller chunks. Regardless of the class, I always made it work by adopting an educative approach and ensuring that I led a positive classroom environment where learning was the central focus.

If there is one piece of golden advice that I seek to pass on to you in this chapter, it is to spend time and effort focusing on developing and practising routines well – especially for entering and exiting the classroom safely and respectfully. Trust me, it is worth it, as it helps reiterate to students that you have high expectations of them.

Transitions

Transitions can be challenging for many students. Giving students a clear idea of when you will all move on to the next activity, and how this is to be done, can help establish a positive classroom culture and maximise learning. In fact, getting transitions right may just be the best time-saver you can employ as a teacher. It also can make your classrooms more inclusive. For some students, especially those with autism, ADHD and other sensory processing disorders, transitions between activities and the associated noise and disorder can be difficult, and this can lead to challenging behaviours.

The most efficient way to transition between activities is to first use a cue to stop the students and to gain their attention – a strategy that I call a 'call to arms'. A call to arms can be verbal or non-verbal. A non-verbal example is simply raising your hand in the air, which signifies to students that it is almost time for you to give an instruction. You can couple this with an audible response, too. For example, you might teach the students that as soon as you raise your hand, they are to make a 'shhh' sound. As one student sees and responds with the audible cue, other students follow and all of a sudden the whole class is tuned in and ready to receive instruction for a transition. Enacting a call to arms is much better than talking over students and getting them to move between activities while some are still working.

The 'when I, you' strategy is great as a verbal call to arms:

When I [say, do, put] _____, you [move, say, stop, look etc.]

For example:

- 'When I *put my hands on my head,* you *look at Mr Hudson.*'
- 'When I say *'waterfall',* you say *'shhh.'*'

Again, this strategy needs to be explicitly taught and practised. The execution of this strategy relies on you giving the students a cue, to which they respond with a certain reply. You then wait for a desired result, which, in most cases, will be eyes on you and everyone being still and focused.

Once you have gained the students' attention, you affirm the students:

> 'Great, thank you to those students who did that so quickly. I can see that all eyes are on me. Can I ask that you put down all materials please and keep your eyes on me. You should have nothing in your hands. We are now almost ready to move to the next activity.'

After this, you deliver a similar prompt focused on what the students need to do next. You can do this using the movement, action, task (MAT) approach, and then seek understanding. For example:

> 'When I say 'go', you are going to walk slowly back to your desk [movement]. You are then going to take out your journal and a pen [action]. You will start writing the introduction to your narrative story [task]. If you understand what you need to do, please put one hand in the air. If you do not know what to do, place two hands in the air.'

At this point, you may choose to explain what needs to happen again to clear up confusion, or allow the students to ask a question. Alternatively, if only a few students need extra help, you might say 'go' so that most students can continue with the transition to the next task, and then offer individualised support to the students who need it.

Here are some transition tips that you can use to ensure students move in an orderly way between activities:

- Prepare students first. Given them fair warning of when an activity will soon end and that in, say, two minutes the class will be transitioning to another activity. This ensures that the students know what is coming up.
- Use a visual timer or a countdown system if you have the means in your classroom. This is especially important for transitions that require students to clean up before moving to another activity.
- Maintain consistency with how you approach transitions in class. Ensure that all students know what is expected of them and assist students who need more clarification and modelling.
- Remain calm and supportive when students are transitioning. Focus on what the student is doing right. Offer assistance in the form of positive and constructive feedback, such as 'Peter, I can see that you have moved to your desk, which is great, but you don't have your book out yet. Can you please take out your book and continue on with the task that was set.'

Use an educative mindset to adapt to context

Engages in precorrection

Establishes behavioural expectations in the classroom

Precorrection is a preventative practice strategy that sees the teacher describing the expectations for the upcoming task or movement. It is often implemented when the teacher has noticed students often struggle to start, perform or complete a certain activity without off-task behaviour occurring.

Precorrection starts with the teacher identifying the context in which a problem behaviour is likely to occur. This is then relayed back to the students, and prompts are provided to reinforce expected behaviours. In essence, precorrection is a strategy that proactively addresses off-task behaviour before it occurs by providing students with support to complete the task or movement in more appropriate ways. Precorrection is often coupled with BSP for maximum effect.

The steps to implement precorrection are as follows:

1. Identify the predictable off-task behaviour and the context in which it is most likely to occur.
2. Identify the expected behaviour, and specify to students what is acceptable and what is not, and why this is the case.
3. Modify the context in which the off-task behaviour is most likely to occur. This may mean modifying the classroom layout or trying new pedagogical approaches to learning.
4. Provide precorrective prompts to students related to the behaviour that is being focused on.
5. Practise and model the expected behaviour with and alongside students.
6. Provide BSP to students who are engaging in corrective behaviours and support students who need extra assistance.
7. Monitor progress and provide feedback to students.

Let's now look at a practical example of precorrection in action.

Context

Susan, a Year 7 Science teacher, notices that several of her students are disrupting others' learning when they are working in groups during practical science experiments. The students in question often walk over to other groups and purposefully interfere with their experiments. Susan finds that she has to repeatably remind her students to focus on their own experiment and not interfere with others.

Susan has this class twice a week. She has noticed that the off-task behaviour occurs mostly on Friday after lunch, when she facilitates practical sessions. It does not happen when she has the class on Tuesday morning for theory lessons.

Expected behaviour

Susan determines that she would like her students to work productively in groups on Friday afternoons like they do on Tuesday mornings. She would like to see all groups afforded the opportunity to undertake the practical activities to their best of their ability and without disruption to their learning. She explicitly states this to the students the next time she sees them.

Modifications

Susan writes the classroom expectations on the whiteboard at the front of the classroom in large font. She brings the students' attention to these at the start of each lesson as a reminder of the expected behaviours in class. Underneath these expectations, Susan writes the focus of the precorrection – successfully engaging in practical activities without disruption – below the classroom expectations so that it is on the board and in focus the whole lesson. This is to ensure that students know what the behavioural focus is in that lesson, much like an instructional learning intention and success criteria.

Susan begins to allocate students to groups, whereas in the past they were able to choose their own groups. She also creates specific roles within the groups so that everyone has a task to do, and provides each group with a self-assessment feedback sheet to record how well each member of the team worked in that lesson.

Susan also facilitates a discussion with the class. She asks them why they think they are more likely to engage in off-task behaviour on Friday after lunch. From this discussion, it is established that the students need to undertake a 'do now' activity as soon as they enter the classroom, so that they can switch their attention to the class – which they find difficult after lunch. Susan distributes a 'do now' activity related to the practical activity each Friday, which students get once they walk into the classroom.

Precorrective prompts

Once students are lined up outside of the classroom and ready to enter quietly and calmly, Susan provides them with a reminder prompt to engage in expected behaviours in the lesson. She uses verbal cues, such as, 'Our focus today is ensuring that all students have the opportunity to participate in the practical activities without disruption. We have been doing this well over the last few weeks and

I value the effort that you are all making with this focus.' This, too, is a good time to reinforce the impact of the modifications that have been made and reinforce the positive outcomes that are occurring as a result of the changes.

BSP and cement statements

Susan provides individual students BSP for displaying the expected behaviours and also uses cement statements to small groups and the whole class that reinforce the positive change in the classroom.

The next toolkit focuses on the ecological conditions in the classroom – those that can be directly managed and those that may, at times, require some workarounds.

Toolkit: Ecological management in the classroom

We all know that the learning environment can have a major impact on students' learning progression and engagement. We can think of this in ecological terms with the example of a rainforest. For trees to grow, the conditions need to be right: temperature, rain, humidity and so on. It is the same for behaviour in the classroom. We need to be able, and willing, to adapt and lead our classroom environments so that they match the needs of the students therein, enabling them to grow and flourish as learners. Effective classroom layouts and environmental management structures enable maximum time to be focused on learning, while also supporting students' sense of safety and connectedness. To create such an environment, though, requires us to have a clear vision about:

- what we want our classrooms to look and feel like for ourselves and our students
- how we'd like others to describe the look and feel of the classroom as a guest in the space
- what we want our students to achieve in the lesson
- what we want to achieve in the lesson.

There are many considerations for ecological management in the classroom; I have documented six of the more common considerations in Figure 4.1.

Figure 4.1: Considerations for ecological management in the classroom

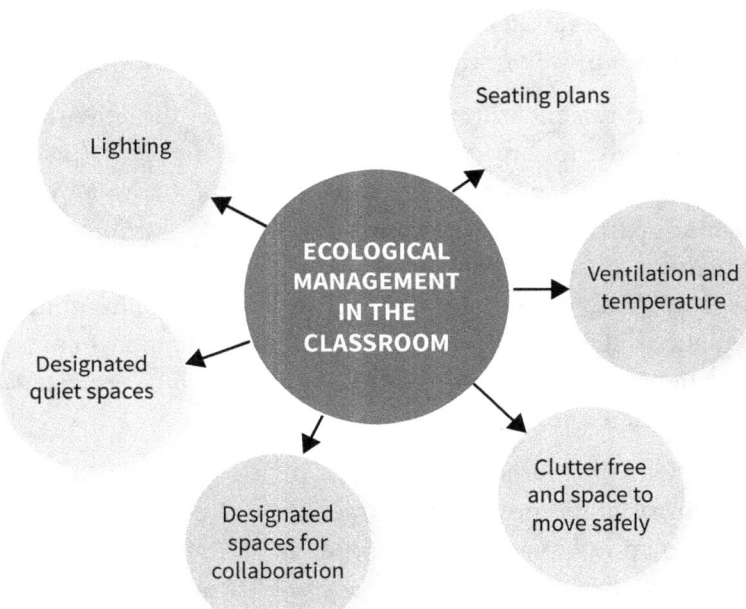

I have often found that lighting, temperature and ventilation coexist and have much impact on students' behaviours in the classroom. For example, on a hot day when students are coming back from lunch, you'd be hard pressed to get them to engage in a highly cognitive task if the classroom feels too hot, is too bright and has no air circulation. This is a recipe for off-task behaviour to occur. We know this for ourselves, too – it is much more difficult for us to engage in learning something when the environmental conditions present as a barrier to us concentrating intently.

In many schools, making changes to classroom lighting, temperature and ventilation is not easy. It can sometimes be impossible without the need for significant capital works to be undertaken. If this is the case, the best action you can take is to make pedagogical changes in the moment. You might need to make space in the lesson for more or less collaboration, quiet reading and brain break activities so that students can achieve the success criteria in the lesson. This is an advantage of flexible learning spaces where there are designated quiet and collaboration areas in the classroom, enabling pedagogical changes to suit the environmental conditions you are working with.

Before each lesson starts, ask yourself: are the environmental conditions right for my rainforest (students) to grow (learn) with what I currently have planned in the lesson? If the answer is no, and you cannot easily change the conditions in the classroom, you might benefit from changing your pedagogical approach – ensuring the focus is still intently on learning but in a slightly different manner than planned. Doing so limits the prevalence of students engaging in off-task behaviours as a result of environmental conditions negatively affecting their ability to focus and engage.

Next we will consider seating plans, which connects strongly to the classroom systems preventative practice, and discuss how they can be used to complement Sutherland et al.'s (2019) practice elements of routines, transitions and the establishment of behavioural expectations in the classroom.

Seating plans

It is all well and good to focus on movement in and out of the classroom, but that is only half of the behavioural expectation recipe. The other half is the students knowing where they need to go once they're in the room. Think of it like sailing: you can plan for getting everyone on the boat safely and methodically, but to actually set sail, those on board need to know where they should be on the boat. There can be quite a lot of time wasted at the start of a lesson if students are floundering around trying to figure out where they are going to sit. This is an element of slight chaos that we can limit through planning order – creating a sense of predictability and calm for students, especially for those who need this the most.

Notwithstanding the obvious notion of students knowing where to go straight away when entering the classroom, seating plans can be used to strategically ensure that certain students sit near each other or do not sit near each other so that learning is enhanced. For example, you can make sure that two talkative students are not seated next to each other, which solves the problem of the two students distracting each other prior to it occurring. You can also consider if a student needs to be seated somewhere specific to support their wellbeing. The class might include several students who are known to work well together and extend each other's learning, so you could seat them together to facilitate collaborative learning processes.

If you already know the students you will be teaching, seating plans are best pre-planned and shown to the students at the very start of the school year. This will coincide with when whole-class expectations are being formed and you are practising basic routines such as entering the classroom. You can leverage the power of knowing your students and be discerning as to where you think each student should sit to maximise learning for the whole class. If it is the first time that you have taught the students, you might mix the seating plan up so that each row or table group (depending upon your classroom set-up) has a balanced gender ratio and different (or shared) interests. Or you might design the plan randomly with the proviso that it will be changed in two weeks' time, which allows you the scope to figure out what needs to change.

Your seating plans might also change depending upon what you are doing in the class. For example, you might have a general seating plan that is enacted for entry into the classroom, and then this might change as students engage in collaborative tasks together. If you're using a specific pedagogical model, such as the Victorian teaching and learning model (Department of Education Victoria, 2023), you might let students know that during the 'explore' phase of the lesson, they are free to sit in different areas of the classroom (this may also include soft pillow areas, or communal spaces in open-planned learning environments) so that they can engage in open collaboration with others. Essentially, the most effective seating plans are those that are tailored to the students' individual learning needs while also being contextual to the content being taught and the physical space available. You can be flexible with how you construct seating plans so long as students know where they are going as soon as they walk into the classroom. This is the most salient benefit of a seating plan: it ensures a sense of order. It creates a common expectation that as soon as everyone enters the classroom, the focus is on learning.

It also helps if you display the seating plan in the classroom as a diagram so that students can understand their positioning in relation to the layout. Students might have several different seating plans as they engage in different subjects, so it is important that a diagram is displayed so that they can visually see where to sit. I have usually displayed this just inside the classroom – that way, if a student is unsure of where their seat is as they greet me when we engage in our entering-the-classroom routine, I refer them to the diagram so that they can see and direct themselves to their seat. You can also use name tents (e.g. folded paper, totems) if you are super organised.

Let's look at a hypothetical example of a teacher, Carla, creating and adapting a seating plan for a new class at the start of the year. Let's say that the first two weeks of Carla's unit on the human body will feature mostly direct instruction, and activities where students will work in pairs. Carla decides to adopt the Central U classroom seating arrangement (Figure 4.2) as this supports, pedagogically, how the start of the unit will be taught.

As this is a new class, and Carla has not met the students yet, she randomly assigns the seats. However, being proactive, Carla has spoken to the year level coordinator for some feedback on the students, and has been advised that Wayne and Jayden should not be seated near each other as they are prone to distracting one another.

Carla then uses the first two lessons to getting to know her students and having them get to know her. She also practises with and alongside the students the expectations of entering the classroom in a safe and orderly manner, while also developing whole-class expectations for learning. With a positive classroom environment in place, Carla moves on to teaching the curriculum.

Figure 4.2: The Central U classroom seating arrangement

```
                    FRONT OF CLASS                      DOOR

                          Carla

   Max           Anna              Lee          Danii

   Nikki         Bec               John         Jayden

                 Sarah             Jed
   Chloe                                        Matt

                 Wayne  Lisa  Jess  Lu

   Sam                                          Rob


   Michael  Mark   Lauren   Tara   Kim   Nat
```

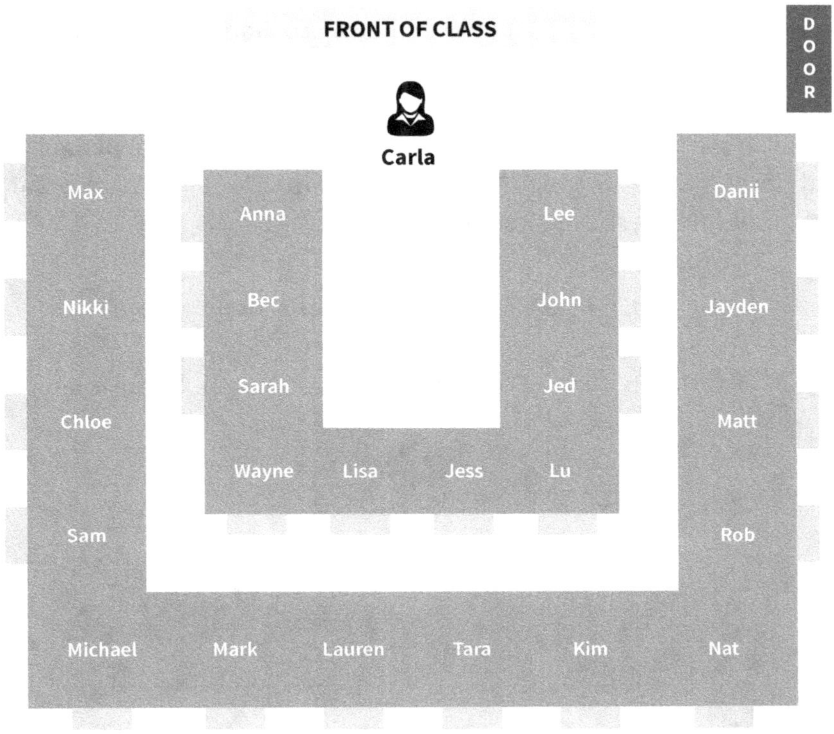

As the unit progresses, Carla changes her pedagogy so that there is less direct instruction and more student-led investigation and collaboration. She has now also seen first-hand how the students interact with one another and has documented who works well together and who needs additional support, as well as critiquing her own practice to better understand how to teach the group in front of her.

To further enhance students' learning for the rest of the unit, Carla decides to change from the Central U classroom seating arrangement to the Mini Us classroom seating arrangement (Figure 4.3). This set-up promotes small-group collaboration, and Carla can position herself in the middle of any of the Us to have targeted discussions with each group, which suits the instructional activities that she has planned for the remainder of the unit. Further, it allows Carla to strategically group students according to her professional acumen so that learning is enhanced for all students. For example, Carla had noticed that in the Central U set-up, Sam, Michael and Mark were often engaging in off-task behaviours each negatively influencing each other's learning. She had also noticed that Sam remained focused when he collaborated with Lisa in learning tasks. Moving to the Mini Us set-up allows Carla to account for these considerations.

Figure 4.3: The Mini Us classroom seating arrangement

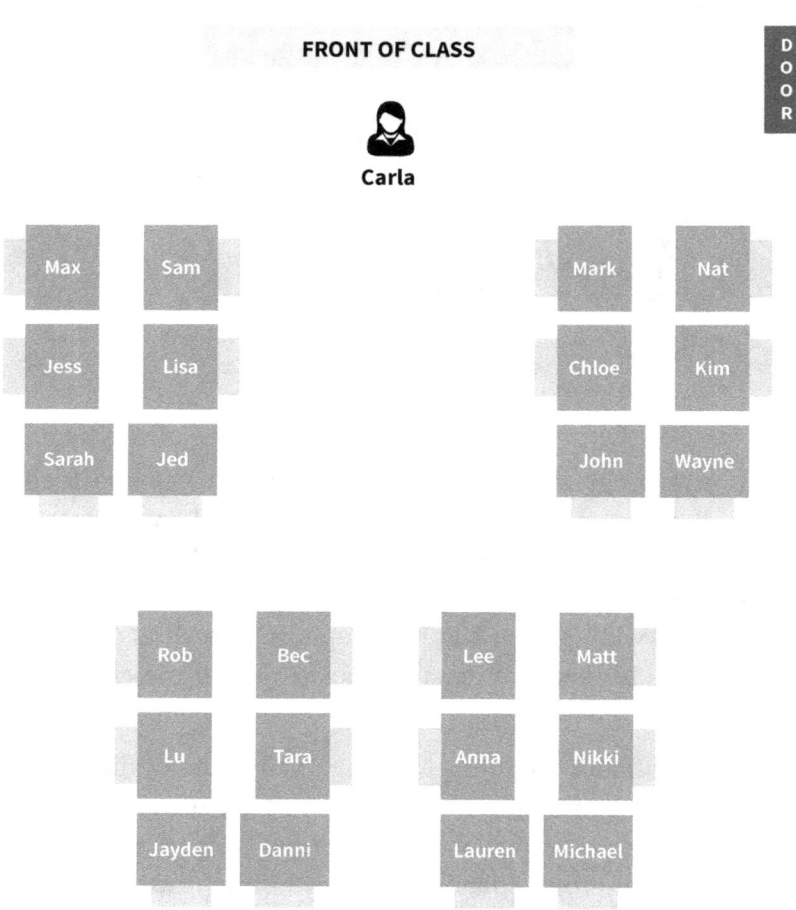

As this is a new seating arrangement for the class, before Carla moves on to the next part of the unit she spends a lesson detailing the new plan and the reason for the change (e.g. because there will be more group work and, importantly, to enhance the learning of everyone in the class). She also practises with the students, once again, how to enter the room safely and methodically and how to find their allocated seat at the start of the lesson. With the new changes established, Carla proceeds to the more collaborative phase of the unit.

While this example demonstrates a change to the classroom set-up, you may not experience this in your own classroom. There are certain classrooms (e.g. a science lab) in which seating structures cannot change; or your school may have an agreed-upon way of arranging the seats and desks in each classroom. There may also be no need for a change in the set-up. The point is that you must work within your own context and what you can and cannot reasonably do within it. In most cases, though, having some sort of seating plan is better than not having one, regardless of the classroom set-up. As a leader of the classroom, it allows you to provide direction to students the moment they walk in, which limits chaos and brings the focus immediately to learning. In my own experience, I have found that it is better to start with order than it is to start with chaos, especially in schools in challenging contexts.

'Do now' activities

It is also valuable for students to have a 'do now' activity to begin as soon as they sit at their desks. A 'do now' is a primer activity that usually takes no longer than five or ten minutes to complete. While they can take some time to prepare, 'do now' activities are incredibly valuable: they ensure that the focus of the lesson is immediately on learning.

You can facilitate a 'do now' in several ways. For example, you can write a prompt up on the board, such as an open-ended or specific question, or a short statement for students to reflect upon. This might relate to the main task in the lesson that day, or it may be a consolidation activity that recaps prior lessons.

Activity options include:

- A quick write – students write a one-paragraph story related to the prompt on the board.
- Design a quiz – students write down as much as they know about the prompt on the board and design a quiz to give to someone else in the class.
- Design a game – students play a game or puzzle to better understand the prompt on the board.

You might also have a stack of 'do now' activity cards just inside the door for students to select from. Or, if you have the time, you might place a 'do now' activity on each student's desk before they enter. They can also be differentiated to suit an individual student's learning needs.

CHAPTER SUMMARY AND REFLECTION

In this chapter we have leveraged the work of Sutherland et al. (2019) to discuss six of the 24 common practice elements that teachers in their study successfully used to promote students' social, emotional and behavioural development. I discussed these seven practices in relation to four preventative practice strategies that you can use in your teaching alongside the adoption of an educative approach to behaviour management. While not exhaustive, these four preventative practice strategies provide you with a solid base, allowing you to focus on prevention over management, which is important when seeking to lead positive classrooms.

Take a moment now to reflect on your learning and understanding through the *tomorrow, next week, beyond* thinking tool, which is best used in dialogue with a mentor or critical friend. It will help you commit to embedding the key preventative practice strategies discussed in this chapter into your practice.

- **Tomorrow:** What commitment can you make to embed one or more of the preventative practice strategies in your teaching tomorrow?

- **Next week:** What commitment can you make to embed one or more of the preventative practice strategies in your teaching next week?
- **Beyond:** What commitment can you make to embed one or more of the preventative practice strategies beyond next week?

CHAPTER 5

CORRECTION STRATEGIES

*'Because you believed I was capable of behaving decently,
I did.' – Paulo Coelho*

Correction strategies are those that are needed in the moment to change the course of a student's off-task behaviours. In terms of walking the wire, they are what you do in the middle of the wire. For many teachers, this can be the scariest place to be, because it often involves a certain level of conflict. We all try to avoid conflict, but it's important to recognise that conflict is an opportunity for positive change. In the context of this book, conflict is where we have much opportunity to adopt an educative approach to behaviour management.

Mahatma Gandhi, an Indian lawyer who promoted nonviolence, remarked, 'Peace is not the absence of conflict, but the ability to cope with it.' In many classrooms, conflict might be inevitable. But, as leaders of positive classrooms, it is up to us to positively use conflict as a means for adaptation – a space of learning where growth occurs for both ourselves and our students.

I'll begin the chapter by introducing my 5 Rs whole-school behaviour education model. Next, we'll consider the importance of delivering engaging lessons that cater for all students' learning needs. I'll discuss the effective use of hinting techniques as a means of correcting students' off-task behaviours in the first instance. Then we'll consider the first four stages of the model – reminder, restate, reposition and relocation. The chapter concludes with a scenario-based reflection activity that invites you to think about how you would respond in relation to the behaviour education model presented.

Chapter learning intentions

By the end of this chapter, you will be able to:

- promote a whole-school approach to behaviour education in your school
- enact four hinting strategies that invite students to self-correct off-task behaviour
- adopt a scaled response to behaviour education in your classroom
- reflect on how you might enact a scaled response in relation to four scenarios.

A whole-school approach to behaviour education

Consistency is an essential part of the behaviour education approach – not only consistency within your own practice, but across the whole school. Students require stable learning environments with clear and consistent expectations. They must be aware of the boundaries of what is appropriate behaviour and what is not. Although you will have developed your own whole-class expectations for learning (Chapter 4), there must also be an element of consistency that extends across the whole school. It is confusing for a student to enter a classroom that has firm and fair boundaries in place, only to enter a classroom with no boundaries in the very next lesson. The water gets murky when there a school lacks consistency, and we cannot blame students for engaging in off-task behaviours when they are confused about what is expected.

Most schools will have a whole-school approach to managing behaviour as part of their policies, but I have often found there is often a large disconnect between what is written in those policies and what is enacted in classrooms. To prepare for this book, I read hundreds of behaviour management policies and I found many to be confusing and opaque. Very few of the policies included models that spoke to everyone in the school community so that there would be a common understanding of expectations for learning in the school. Most of the policies I viewed focused only on managing incidents, as opposed to tying together pedagogical changes and a scaled management response. Many didn't make sense at all, and seemed to have been written as a tick-box exercise rather than with any real thought. I concluded that if *I* was confused reading some of these policies, how could we expect *students* to understand the expectations?

How can teachers achieve consistency of practice if their behaviour management policies don't make sense? How can they be supported to lead positive classrooms if these policies are almost impossible to transfer over to practical on-the-ground settings? I found consistency to be a huge gap in several of the behaviour management policies that I perused. This is an important consideration for school leaders who are reading this book. In their study of how teacher attrition has impacted the work of three Australian teachers in the hardest-to-staff schools, Lampert et al. (2023) found that the teachers felt competent to manage students' off-task behaviours if supportive organisational systems and practices were in place – for example, assistance from school leadership if needed as a specifically defined scaled response. If adequate structures are not in place, teachers go without this assistance and guidance and are forced to navigate the 'sinking ship' (Lampert et al., 2023) of behaviour management by themselves. The deck of cards collapses in on itself.

To counter this, and to set the scene for the remainder of the chapter, I'll provide you with my own version of a whole-school approach to behaviour education that your school can adopt. I present this in a schematic model – my 5 Rs whole-school behaviour education model (Figure 5.1). Schools and student behaviour are both complex, and schematic models help us make sense of complexity so that a common understanding is reached. Schematic models provide us with clarity, and clarity is the base for consistency. If all teachers and students are on the same page with a consistent approach to behaviour education, the entire school community benefits.

You may wish to change elements of this model to suit your own school context, but the most important factor is that everyone understands what the approach actually is. This helps build a collective belief that the approach to behaviour education between classrooms is clear, consistent and to the benefit of students' learning.

Figure 5.1: The 5 Rs whole-school behaviour education model

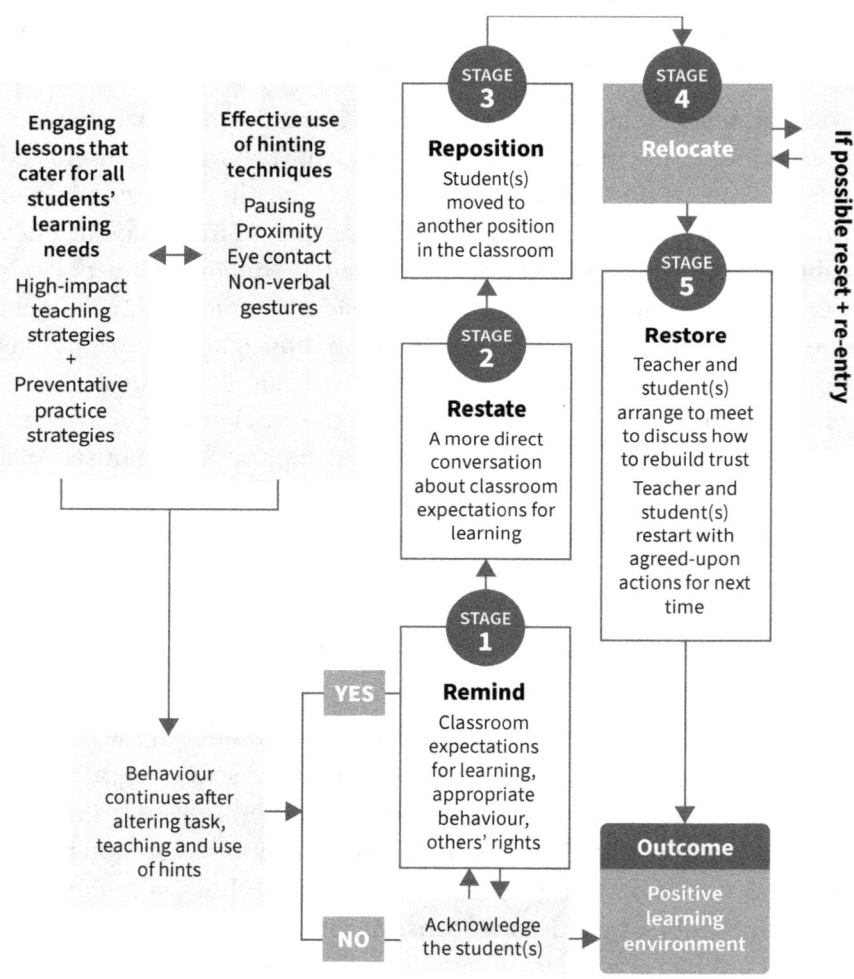

Supported by high-growth relationships with students = referent power

Build trust and show genuine care
Get to know students as individuals
What are your students' interests outside of school?

Have a sense of humour
What interests do you share with your students?
What are your students' life goals?

The model is underpinned by the premise that your aim as the teacher is to establish a positive learning environment for all students. You achieve this by building high-growth relationships with students and establishing referent power (Chapter 1). A positive learning environment is further supported by you delivering engaging lessons that cater for all students' learning needs and through the use of preventative practice strategies (Chapter 4).

More often than not, when the lesson is engaging (that is, learning tasks are within the student's zone of proximal development, the student sees relevance in the learning tasks and the student can work towards mastery) and high-growth relationships have been established, there is a sense of calm enjoyment in the classroom. This is further enhanced by preventative practice strategies such as well-developed classroom routines and well-managed transitions. However, given the complexity of behaviour that we discussed in Chapters 2 and 3, teachers also need to address instances where students engage in off-task behaviours despite our best efforts. The middle of the model speaks to this complexity and provides you with a way in which to *lead* positive classrooms.

The responses within the model are scaled through five separate stages (the 5 Rs) – remind, restate, reposition, relocate and restore – with an additional process to allow for students who have been relocated to reset and re-enter the classroom if this is possible. The escalation of the 5 Rs establishes higher-intensity responses as the off-task behaviour continues, and as the student has been given ample opportunity for change. It is important to adopt this scaled approach, because going from zero to 100 is not appropriate nor reflective of the high-growth relationships you have built with your students. If a student is talking to another student at the back of the classroom while the lesson is being delivered, it is not justifiable for you to exit that student from the classroom as a first response. That is a rather punitive approach, and we need to move well beyond that style. The student needs to be given an opportunity to correct the off-task behaviour themselves, and, if this doesn't occur, then they may need more support in which to do so. This is what it means to adopt a behaviour education approach in our classrooms.

The 5 Rs represent a closed feedback loop whereby if a relocation is enacted, there is an opportunity for the teacher and the student to come together to rebuild trust and agree upon ways to move forward in their relationship so that a positive classroom environment is maintained. The restore stage is discussed further in Chapter 6. In most classrooms, changes to pedagogy, the effective use of hinting techniques, and the first three stages of the 5 Rs will suffice. We'll explore all of these next.

Engaging lessons that cater for all students' learning needs

Before we delve into the strategies that you can employ to correct off-task behaviours in your classroom, I'd like to direct you back to what we discussed in Chapter 1. Often, the most powerful thing that we can do as practitioners to limit off-task behaviour is change our pedagogy so that students find meaning and joy in what they are learning. This is central to having high expectations for students' learning and is a core component of establishing high-growth relationships with students.

I have often seen classrooms in which off-task behaviour is rife, where students are given worksheets or told to work from textbooks with little to no deviation. To me, in this scenario, off-task behaviour is to be expected. Students will find ways to entertain themselves if they are bored and disengaged.

While instructional practices are not the core focus of this book (perhaps that will be the next book!) simply asking ourselves the question, 'What can I do *differently* to engage *all* students in this class more meaningfully?' allows for more inclusive, fun and engaging pedagogy to enter our practice. Get creative! Think outside the box! How else can you deliver content related to the topic? Lean in to your high-growth relationships with students and leverage their interests so that content is connected with what they are passionate about. You might just find that changing your pedagogical approach is by far the most powerful preventative mechanism to limit off-task behaviour.

The Department of Education Victoria's *High Impact Teaching Strategies* (2023) offer guidelines for making lessons more engaging. The ten suggested high-impact teaching strategies (HITS) are:

1. setting goals
2. structuring lessons
3. explicit teaching
4. worked examples
5. collaborative learning
6. multiple exposures
7. questioning
8. feedback
9. metacognitive strategies
10. differentiation teaching.

The HITS have emerged from the findings of tens of thousands of studies on enhancing student learning outcomes in classrooms across Australia and the world (Department of Education Victoria, 2023). They are a bank of reliable and evidence-informed practices that you can use to better connect students with their learning. If students are engaging in off-task behaviours in your classroom, it might of benefit to consult the HITS and consider tweaks to your pedagogy. The use of HITS is supported further by the preventative practice strategies as detailed in Chapter 4.

The following sections focus on corrective strategies that can be employed in addition to changes to pedagogy and preventative practices.

Toolkit: Correcting off-task behaviour with hinting techniques

Hinting techniques usually precede more formal interventions, making students aware that their off-task behaviour needs to change (Lewis, 2008; Lewis et al., 2005). They are 'soft' prompts that give students an opportunity to self-correct their behaviour. In their study, Lewis et al. (2005) found that students perceived the classroom environment to be more positive when their teachers used hinting strategies as a first port of call to manage off-task behaviour. The use of hinting techniques 'related to a stronger belief [from students] that the discipline actions taken by the teacher were warranted'.

Four of the more common hinting techniques that teachers can use as part of their practice are:

- pausing
- proximity
- eye contact
- non-verbal signs.

These four techniques are generally used in conjunction with one another. Examples of how they might be used in your classroom are detailed following.

Hinting combination one: pausing and eye contact

Pausing is an interruption of instructional action and is generally associated with another hinting technique: eye contact. This technique is generally used when students are talking while you're delivering instruction in the lesson. Rather than continue delivering instruction, perhaps even speaking louder to drown out the talking students' voices, a slight pause is often all that is needed.

While it is always tempting to fill an awkward silence, enacting a pause and staying in the moment is often a powerful agent for change. When a pause is coupled with eye contact, it signifies to the class where that distraction is coming from. This creates a sense of community influence on the off-task behaviour, as the distraction is not just between the teacher and the student, but also between the student and their classmates. The key to this technique is avoiding holding eye contact for too long as it can become a 'stare-off' challenge. Slide your eyes away from the student once they have resumed on-task behaviour.

Example

Johnny and Max are laughing and talking with each other at the back of the class while the teacher, Mark, is explaining the next steps in the learning task. The rest of the students are listening intently. Mark pauses his instruction and makes eye contact with both Johnny and Max, signifying to them that their off-task behaviour is disruptive. Johnny and Max realise that instruction has stopped for the whole class and so they correct their own behaviour, and Mark continues his instruction.

A scaled iteration

An iteration of this technique can include cement statements (Chapter 4). If Mark has stopped his instruction and both Johnny and Max are continuing to talk and have not yet realised Mark is making eye contact, Mark might also use a scaled cement statement to support the hinting strategy. This statement acknowledges other students' on-task behaviour and further draws attention to the off-task behaviour of Johnny and Max. For example, Mark might say something like:

> 'I can see that most of the class is listening intently to the instructions for the next learning task. Thank you to everyone who is doing so. We will, however, have to stop for a moment so that everyone in the class can join us. Johnny and Max, you are currently talking between yourselves and this is disrupting others' learning. You need to stop talking and pay attention to the instructions that I am giving. Thank you both for doing this.'

You will see that this cement statement is scaled from the broad to the local. First, there is recognition of those in the class who are on-task and engaging in desired behaviours. Second, there is targeted commentary provided to both Johnny and Max. This is achieved by acknowledging what the off-task behaviour is, the effect it is having on others, and what the two students need to do to correct the behaviour. Last, a public acknowledgement is provided to the two students in advance for changing their behaviour. Johnny and Max now know what they need to do for self-correction.

Hinting combination two: proximity and non-verbal gestures

Proximity relates to the use of the teacher's body in the space of the classroom. Often, we think that we need to be the sage on the stage and deliver instruction at the front of the classroom. This invites pockets of off-task behaviours to occur as the distance between the teacher and students increases. In traditional classrooms of rowed seating, the off-task behaviour usually occurs at the back of the classroom. This is one reason I dislike rowed seating. I believe it is important to change learning spaces up so that they are more collaborative, engaging and invite creativity.

Changes to learning spaces can allow for a more even spread of distance between the teacher and each student. For example, if the teacher is delivering direct instruction in a lesson, a horseshoe-shaped set-up allows for the teacher to move between from the front of the horseshoe all the way down the middle while doing so. This keeps all of the students' eyes on the teacher and limits the distance between the teacher and any one student. This sense of closeness deters students from engaging in off-task behaviours.

A teacher can also deploy the strategy of proximity in other ways besides making changes to learning spaces. I will use the same example of Johnny and Max to illustrate this.

Example

Johnny and Max are laughing and talking with each other at the back of the class while the teacher, Mark, is explaining the next steps in the learning task. The rest of the students are listening intently. Mark continues his delivery of instruction and moves from the front of the class to the back of the class and positions himself next to Johnny and Max. His proximity signifies to them that their behaviour is disruptive. Johnny and Max realise that Mark is now positioned close to them and that their behaviour needs to change. With the off-task behaviour now corrected, Mark continues with the instruction and positions himself elsewhere in the classroom.

A scaled iteration

An iteration of this technique can include the use of non-verbal signs. If Mark has positioned himself next to Johnny and Max and they are continuing to talk, Mark might use a non-verbal hand gesture such as raising his hand and displaying an open palm to both students while still explaining the instruction to the rest of the class. Alternatively,

Mark might use the table-tapping technique, which sees him use four fingers to tap the table three times. This signifies to both students that they need to stop talking. Johnny and Max are now aware that their behaviour is disruptive and what they need to do for self-correction.

If the off-task behaviour ceases after a hinting strategy has been used, it is important to make space in the lesson to speak to the students and acknowledge the self-correction and positive change in behaviour. This is an important consideration for building and leading learning environments. In the scenario that has been described above, once Mark has finished his instructions and the class is engaging in the learning task, he might approach Johnny and Max and acknowledge them further. For example:

> 'Johnny and Max, I had to stop the lesson before because you were both talking and it was disrupting others' learning. You recognised this and you both stopped immediately. Thank you. This allowed me to continue on with the instructions that I was giving to the class. How are you both going with the task? Is there anything that I can help you with?'

In this statement, Mark has, once again, labelled the off-task behaviour that Johnny and Max were engaging in and also the effect that it had on others. After this, he acknowledges the change that occurred (the talking stopped). Next, he gives praise to the students and explains the effect of the behaviour change (Mark was able to continue with his instruction). Last, he brings the conversation back to the learning task at hand and offers assistance to enhance the students' engagement with the task. This statement demonstrates to the students that Mark has, simultaneously, a high expectation for their learning and a high amount of care – the central tenets of high-growth relationships.

 **Toolkit: Correcting off-task behaviour with the 5 Rs**

If pedagogical changes, preventative practice strategies and hinting techniques are not working and the off-task behaviour is continuing, the model provides scope for you to move through multiple escalation stages to correct the behaviour. These stages also provide students ample opportunity for self-correction. Table 5.1 explains each stage of the 5 Rs.

Table 5.1: Moving through the 5 Rs

Stage	Elaboration
1. Remind	• Raise students' behavioural awareness and remind them of the expected behaviour inside the classroom. • Achieved through a direct affective statement using the AID technique, the four question strategy or peer prompting. • Consider conducting an educative conversation with students in relation to why the behaviour has occurred and the steps that need to be taken for the student to engage with the lesson (e.g. more explanation, differentiation etc.).
2. Restate	• Remind students of the previous reminder. Remind them of the natural consequences that ensue at Stage 3. • Conduct an educative conversation with students and formally direct them to the school's values and/or the whole-class expectations for learning, investigating which one of the values is not being adhered to and why, and the effect of their behaviour on others. • Redirect students to the learning task and provide assistance as needed.
3. Reposition	• Remind students of the previous reminders and formally direct them to the school's values and/or the whole-class expectations for learning. • Conduct an educative conversation with students in relation to which one of the values is not being adhered to and why, and the effect of their behaviour on others. • Advise students that their behaviour is an ongoing concern for their and others' learning and, as such, you will reposition them elsewhere in the classroom.

Stage	Elaboration
4. Relocate	- Advise students they will be relocated without the audience of the rest of the class. - Provide students a reflection sheet for them to fill in. This will inform the restorative justice conversation to repair harm and rebuild relationships (Step 5). - If appropriate, provide an opportunity for the student to re-enter the classroom after a resetting period. - Before the end of the day, phone parents to explain the behaviour that led to the relocation, and the steps taken to rectify the behaviour prior to it. Explain what will be done to rebuild and repair the relationships.
5. Restore	- Meet with students to explore their side of the story. It is important that students are given the opportunity to explain their thoughts, feelings and actions. This might mean providing prompts to the students so that they are able to see the connection between their thoughts, feelings and actions. - Explore the harm that has been caused and unpack who has been affected by it. - Repair the harm so that everyone affected can move forward positively, either in that moment or reach an agreement on how to move forward positively over time. Note: In many schools, this conversation is conducted by someone other than the classroom teacher, e.g. a coordinator or assistant principal, as a result of a 'referral'. It is important that if the harm is between a teacher and a student, the teacher is brought into the conversation at this point. As Lewis et al. (2005) framed it, 'teachers cannot allow themselves and difficult students to be locked into a vicious cycle of reciprocal causation' and there is much benefit from involving teachers in restorative justice conversations with students – it builds high-growth relationships.

Stage 1: Remind

Stage 1 will see you raise students' behavioural awareness and remind them of the expected behaviour inside the classroom. You can utilise the four-question technique, the peer prompting technique or the action, impact, do/do differently (AID) technique to influence a positive change in behaviour. Let's look at the three techniques now.

The four-question technique

This technique is a simple, structured questioning strategy that raises a student's behavioural awareness. When a student is off-task with their learning, and the use of hinting techniques has not been effective, engage in dialogue with the student through four sequential questions:

1. What are you doing?
2. What should you be doing?
3. What is stopping you from doing what you should be doing?
4. What can we do together to get you back on track with your learning?

Quite often we ask students questions about their behaviour but we often miss one very important ingredient: the final question which involves us working with the student to solve the problem. For example, we might say:

> 'Nicholas, why on earth are you doing that? Knock it off, mate!'

While this might bring Nicholas' attention to whatever it is he is doing (behaviour awareness), there really isn't a next step. Nicholas can either stop the behaviour or he can keep doing it. When I have coached staff in the past, I've found that if Nicholas were to keep going with the behaviour it is almost always followed by something like this:

> 'Nicholas, I've asked you once and I am not going to do it again. Keep going and you are with me after school.'

Cue the lure of coercive power.

Now, Nicholas can either stop or he can keep going, but he now has a threat of punishment in front of him in a public forum. This might work, but then again it might escalate the behaviour further; this depends on what Nicholas is trying to 'access' and/or 'avoid' (see Chapter 2). We want to avoid further escalation but we also want to change the behaviour, and the four-question strategy allows for this to occur. When strung together, the four questions raise the behaviour awareness of the student and they offer, through dialogue, the opportunity to seek a collaborative solution: how are *we* going to get you back on track with *your* learning? As mentioned, we often miss that part and search for a quick fix – a coercive statement. I get it. With 25 other students in the class you might feel the need to go there. But if you instead make space for dialogue with the student, often the solution is right there – for example, differentiation, further support, another explanation of the learning task, providing materials etc. The four-question technique may sound simple but it is a great one to add to your teacher toolbelt when leading for behaviour in your classroom.

The peer prompting technique

This technique is a way to redirect a student's off-task behaviour without having to speak to the student directly about the behaviour. Sometimes you may feel like you're dealing with the same student over and over again. My message here is that, sometimes, it is not necessary to address the student's behaviour directly. Peer prompting raises a student's behavioural awareness through social modelling.

For example, let's say Aisha is off-task and talking to the student to her right, but the student on her left, Ruby, is working diligently on her numeracy task.

One option is to address Aisha directly, but there is another way of getting Aisha back on task with her learning without addressing her off-task behaviour directly (such as through the four-question technique). Using peer prompting, you could compliment Ruby on how well she's working.

'Ruby, I can see that you're concentrating really hard there. I'll be over in a minute to see the great work you're doing.'

In some cases, a peer prompting statement such as this is enough to change the student's off-task behaviour and get them back on task with their learning, especially if they know that you are coming over to their table group soon (proximity). It raises students' behavioural awareness by drawing their attention to an example of the behaviour they should be displaying.

Here are some tips for using the peer prompting technique:

- Make the prompt short and sharp.
- Add a timed element to the prompt, e.g. 'I will be over in a minute.'
- Once you have checked the on-task student's work, follow up with the off-task student to see if they need assistance with their learning.

The AID technique

This technique will see you issue a *direct affective statement* to students to help them see the impact of their off-task behaviour and what needs to happen next. It is an easy-to-remember behavioural change technique that I learnt during my time as a Constable for Victoria Police. We were taught to use this method to in communication with the public in a positive, non-confrontational way. As much as it is a policing method, it can also be used in schools and other organisations. It is a structured and holistic way to deliver performance-based feedback to others, while also ensuring that the feedback given is constructive and drives positive change. Although I use the AID technique here to explain how to drive change in a student's off-task behaviour, it can just as easily be used to provide positive feedback to students on the on-task behaviours they are displaying as part of delivering BSP (Chapter 4).

The three steps of the AID technique are as follows:

- **Action:** acknowledge the student and detail the behaviour

- **Impact:** explain the impact of the behaviour on their own and others' wellbeing and learning
- **Do/do differently:** explicitly and clearly state what needs to happen to correct the behaviour, or outline the behaviour that needs to occur for the student to be successful. This can also be linked to one or several of the whole-class expectations. Provide assistance to the student as needed.

Let's look at an example of how you might use a direct affective statement through the AID technique during Stage 1.

Make sure that when you approach students you adopt the 'horizon stance', where you meet the student at their level. For example, if the student is seated, you will also sit or crouch down so you can lock eye contact at a mutual level. This is important, because direct affective statements need to be delivered from a position of equality and not from a position of power such as when you are standing over a student.

You might say something like:

> 'Hi Sarah. When you got up out of your seat and went over to the door and started yelling loudly, the rest of the students in the class stopped the conversations they were having in their groups in relation to the learning task today. I feel concerned that you are not engaged in the task and your actions are disrupting others' learning. I need you to stay seated at your own table group, engage in the discussion, and continue on with the learning task. Is there anything that I can do to help you be successful with this?'

In this example, Sarah might respond that she genuinely went over to the door for a valid reason. This is an educative opportunity and is part of the power of Stage 1. You might engage in further dialogue with Sarah while also enacting the skill of empathetic listening. You can acknowledge the intended purpose of the action while also asking Sarah community influence and problem-solving questions, giving her the chance to reflect on the effects of her behaviour. For example:

- **Acknowledgement and empathetic listening:** 'Thanks for explaining why you went to the door, Sarah. I understand that you saw Nathan walking past and you wanted to remind him about basketball training after school.'

- **Engage in dialogue through community influence questions:** 'While I can see that you had good intentions there, how do you think getting up out of your seat, opening the door and yelling loudly at Nathan affected others in the class? What about other people in the surrounding classrooms?'
- **Engage in dialogue through problem-solving questions:** 'How else could you have approached the situation? Who could you have asked for help if you needed it?'

If all students in the class are aware of the 5 Rs model they will self-correct their off-task behaviours after Stage 1. In fact, I would confidently say that if you have built referent power with them through the establishment of high-growth relationships, and you are providing them with meaningful and engaging learning tasks that are differentiated to their learning needs, then 90 per cent of off-task behaviours will be corrected or self-corrected through the actions that occur up to and including Stage 1. The remaining stages account for the remaining 10 per cent of situations when more targeted assistance is required.

Stage 2: Restate

Stage 2 (restate) is much the same as Stage 1 (remind); the main difference is that it includes a more formalised redirection to the school's values or the whole-class expectations for learning that have been developed.

Again adopting the horizon stance, the first part of the conversation is a statement that alerts the student that they have already been reminded about the expectations in the classroom and they have now progressed to the second stage of the 5 Rs. You should also remind them of the natural consequence that ensue at Stage 3 – being repositioned somewhere else in the classroom. It is important to be very explicit about this so that the student knows which stage they're at in the 5 Rs. The conversation then centres on what needs to happen for the student to engage in the learning task. The conversation might occur as follows:

- **Reminder of the behaviour and expectations, and acknowledgement of where the student is in the 5 Rs:** 'Hi Sarah. You have been up out of your seat multiple times now heading over to the door and yelling out which is interrupting your own and others' learning. I've already reminded you of the expected behaviour in the lesson. The next time we speak together about this issue I am going to have to move you to another spot in the classroom.'
- **Educative dialogue with the student around the whole-class expectations:** 'Our whole-class expectations are that we show we are organised by devoting maximum time to learning in each class, and we show respect by allowing others to engage in learning without distraction. Which one of these expectations do you feel you aren't meeting at the moment? Why? What effect is it having on your learning? What about the effect on others' learning? How can we correct the behaviour so that you experience success with the learning task while also allowing others to experience success?'
- **Provide assistance:** 'Thanks for your answers and reflections there, Sarah. Now let's work together to get back on track with the lesson. Can you show me where you are up to? Can you explain to me what you have done and what you need to do to ensure that you are meeting the success criteria for the lesson? What can I do to help you meet the success criteria?'

This more formalised stage allows you to provide further assistance to the student so that they can re-engage with the lesson. You might spend five or so minutes working alongside the student, seeking to understand how to better connect them with the learning task at hand. This might also include enacting more targeted use of the HITS (Department of Education Victoria, 2023), such as *worked examples, questioning* or *explicit teaching*.

Stage 3: Reposition

In this stage the student is repositioned in the classroom to further discourage the off-task behaviour. It is, again, important that the student understands where they are within the 5 Rs. There should be no confusion around them having received multiple reminders. The educative dialogue with the student occurs, and then the assistance provided is the movement of them in the classroom so that their own and others' learning can continue.

In Sarah's case, the new position would most definitely not be a seat right next to the door! You might reposition Sarah at the front of the classroom alongside you, which will allow you to provide one-on-one learning support so that Sarah is able to experience success in the lesson. It is also important that Sarah is made aware that the next stage is a relocation out of the classroom and a phone call home to her parents.

If at any point during these first three stages students change their behaviour for the better and engage in on-task behaviours, it is important to acknowledge them through BSP and cement statements (Chapter 4). This builds goodwill and shifts the focus back to the behaviour that you want to see rather than the behaviour that you don't.

Stage 4: Relocate

This stage should only occur when every other option has been reasonably exhausted and there are no other alternatives. You have made three attempts to correct the behaviour, and changed, adapted or differentiated the learning task to engage students in their learning. Students have also been given ample opportunity for self-correction.

It aligns closely with one of Sutherland et al.'s (2019) 24 practice elements detailed in Chapter 4: 'removes student(s) from an activity following the occurrence of misbehaviour'. In relation to low-level off-task behaviours (e.g. disrupting the learning of others through movement and conversational distraction), Stage 4 should occur where the displayed behaviour is a severe detriment to others' learning. If behaviours are considered to be high-level off-task behaviours, such as those that pose a threat to the safety of others (e.g. a physical altercation), this stage might be used as a first port of call. The model allows the scope to target your response according to how your school defines low-level off-task behaviours that warrant a staged approach, and those behaviours that are considered to be high-level dangerous behaviours which warrant the need for immediate relocation.

Stage 4 will look different in each school and is dependent upon the school's capacity to execute it. For example, some schools won't have capacity for other teachers to host students who have been relocated. I'll suggest a few ways that relocation can be achieved.

First, the student is relocated to their respective sub-school office, where one year level coordinator is stationed each period. Second, there is a communal relocation space in the school and this is manned by an assistant principal or lead teacher who is timetabled there for each period as part of their load. Third, there is a reciprocal model in place whereby junior students are relocated to senior classrooms, and senior students are relocated to junior classrooms. It is beneficial if there are wellbeing staff present and available to engage in dialogue with relocated students, especially if co-regulation is needed. It will depend upon how your school is able to structure itself to facilitate a relocation stage for the whole school. However, for the relocation stage to work successfully on a whole-school level, there needs to be some structure in place. If there is no structure, and both teachers and students know that, it will fail. You simply cannot enact Stage 4 without *enabling school structures*, which Gray et al. (2015) defined as teachers' belief that the leadership and structures of the school help support them in their work. Enabling school structures requires consideration of time, space, resources (human and otherwise) and policies that support a whole-school behaviour education model, specifically the ability for Stage 4 to occur if needed.

The most important factor of a relocation is what the student does when they are relocated. Certainly, and I must emphasise this strongly, this is *not* a detention or a punitive measure designed to elicit suffering in the student. It is an opportunity to reflect on behaviour and ascertain what needs to be done in order for the student to continue on with learning. There is absolutely no merit in having relocated students sitting in a room, staring at a wall. That serves no purpose at all and it is not indicative of having high-growth relationships with students.

It is also dangerous to use relocation as a means to belittle and chastise the student who has been relocated. It is, most importantly, a chance to connect with the student and reflect together about the behaviour and the relocation, engaging in dialogue and co-regulation so that the student can return to the classroom as quickly as possible and re-engage with their learning.

One of the best ways to do this is to reify the student's thinking through a reflection sheet, which they can fill in to provide their side of the story in relation to the relocation and any further information that they may wish to provide in a restorative justice conversation between themselves and the teacher. An example of a reflection sheet that I developed as a year level coordinator, and that you and your school can now use, is provided in Figure 5.2. Ideally, this reflection sheet is filled in by the relocated student in dialogue with a teacher and/or a member of the wellbeing team. There is an ethic of care shown towards the student and a genuine desire to understand their version of events. Most importantly, if the student is heightened, it is important that a staff member allocated to relocations assists the student to regulate, and recognise, their emotions and to explain how they are feeling and why.

The 5 Rs model includes an additional process that may be enacted to return the student to the classroom after they have been relocated. If the relocated student has had the opportunity to *reset*, which will often include an element of co-regulation, and they have had the opportunity to fill in a reflection sheet in dialogue with another staff member (wellbeing or otherwise), there is an opportunity for the student to *re-enter* the classroom if it is deemed possible and appropriate. This doesn't mean that Stage 5 (restore) doesn't occur between the student and the teacher – it most definitely still will – but it enables the student the opportunity to re-engage with their learning – the core business of schools. There are times, though, where this just isn't possible. For example, there might only be five minutes left in the lesson; the student may remain in a heightened state with more co-regulation needed; or it may have been a physical incident which means it's inappropriate to return the student to the classroom until parents have been called and a statement of events has been documented. It is best to use your own judgement as to whether or not it is appropriate for a relocated student to re-enter the same lesson. If it isn't appropriate, the student should focus on co-regulation, reflection and/or continue with their learning task in a separate space and with additional support. If it is appropriate, and the student is once again ready to learn, the student can be escorted back to the classroom. The accompanying staff member would then mediate a re-entry conversation between the teacher and the student. This conversation should occur outside of the classroom and should take no more than a couple of minutes.

Following is a five-step example of how to facilitate a re-entry conversation:

1. **Acknowledgement of behaviour and reflective action:**
   'Hi [teacher]. I have [student] with me and we have just had a productive conversation together about [reason for relocation]. We have had the opportunity to sit down together and think through what has led to the need for a relocation today, and also what [student] [needs/wants/thinks] in order to re-enter the classroom and re-engage successfully with the learning in the remainder of the lesson. We have also filled in a reflection sheet which you can both refer to when you have your restorative justice meeting later on.'
2. **Student voice:** The mediating teacher then allows the student the opportunity to add to the acknowledgement. '[Student], is there anything you would like to add to that?'
3. **Strategies for success:** The mediating teacher then seeks to establish what both the teacher and the student need to do in order to re-enter the classroom and engage in learning successfully. '[Teacher], what needs to happen so that [student] can experience success with their learning in the remainder of the lesson? [Student], what do you need so that you can experience success with your learning in the remainder of the lesson?'

4. **Co-design:** The mediating teacher, the teacher and the student then co-design two to three agreed-upon goals, strategies or actions in order for the re-entry to occur. 'Thank you to you both. Now that we have had the chance to consider what we all need to continue with learning in the remainder of the lesson, let's come up with a couple of strategies that we can do right now so that the rest of the lesson can be a success.' These might be: a further seating change, being paired with a different student, differentiated work, check-ins every five minutes to gauge the student's connection with learning and so on.
5. **Agreement:** All parties agree to what has been discussed and the student re-enters the classroom to re-engage with their learning.

It is up to you and your school context whether you restart the 5 Rs again; or whether a further relocation might be warranted if the same behaviour continues. There also might not be an opportunity for re-entry until a restorative justice conversation between the teacher and student has been had. This will depend upon your individual school's behavioural policy.

Using the example of Sarah, let's say that after all the learning adjustments have been made, and after all the educative conversations have occurred in the first three stages, she continues to make her way to the door to yell out to students walking past. Her behaviour escalates to the point where her off-task behaviour (in this specific lesson) is detrimental to the whole class. The teacher has a conversation with Sarah in private about her having reached the stage of relocation. This conversation is delivered calmly and respectfully with no malice. The teacher advises Sarah that they will have a further restorative-focused conversation together to ascertain ways to positively move forward for the next lesson. Sarah is then accompanied by another student to a designated relocation area, or a coordinator or assistant principal might come to collect Sarah.

While Sarah is in the relocation space, a wellbeing staff member notices that Sarah is quite heightened and visibly frustrated after being relocated, and so guides her through four rounds of box breathing to help regulate her emotions (Chapter 3). After that, Sarah and the wellbeing staff member engage in dialogue around the answers that she provided in her reflection sheet, especially the last question related to what needs to be done to fix the situation. Sarah recognises that she was trying to access attention from students walking past but went about it the wrong way and shows remorse for what has happened in the lesson. After this reflective period, Sarah explains that she is ready to refocus on her learning, recognising that she would benefit from a worked example by the teacher or another student. Sarah and the wellbeing teacher walk back to the classroom and a re-entry conversation is facilitated. As soon as she re-enters, Sarah is seated at the front of the class and successfully engages with the remainder of the lesson using a worked example provided by a student who has finished the work. The teacher acknowledges Sarah's positive change in the remainder of the lesson as she leaves the classroom, while also advising that a follow-up restorative justice conversation will occur shortly.

The answers that Sarah provides in her reflection sheet are also provided to her parents when the teacher phones home to advise of the relocation that occurred that day. This ensures that the teacher is engaging with others within Sarah's mesosystem to promote a more holistic approach to behaviour education (Chapter 2). The conversation with parents focuses on providing a factual account of what happened in the lesson and the steps that occurred prior to the relocation and after it. In the call, the teacher advises parents that there will be a follow-up restorative justice conversation with Sarah to repair the harm and to focus on ways in which to positively engage with learning in the next lesson.

I have seen some teachers opt to inform parents via email rather than a phone call but I do not advocate for this approach. It is much better to talk to parents over the phone or in person (depending upon availability) so that the conversation is more personable and the parent can ask questions and interact with the teacher.

Figure 5.2: An exemplar relocation reflection sheet for students

---

1. What events led to the relocation? What is your story?

2. What classroom expectations were not being upheld? What could you have done differently?

3. What things happened that your teacher might not know about? Check as many boxes as apply below and comment in the space provided.
   - ☐ I needed assistance
   - ☐ I didn't have equipment
   - ☐ I needed food/drink/toilet
   - ☐ I wanted attention
   - ☐ I needed space
   - ☐ Someone was annoying me
   - ☐ Other

4. What can you do to repair the relationships with others affected? (e.g. yourself, your classmates, your teacher.)

Stage 5: Restore

This stage is perhaps the most important in the 5 Rs model. It is premised upon the central tenets of restorative justice, which is a framework that teachers and school leaders can use to create safe and supportive school cultures.

When relationships in our classrooms come under stress – which will inevitably happen – it doesn't mean that those relationships cease. We must seek to move forward positively, together. Having a fair, reasonable and contextually responsive process in place allows the opportunity for everyone to share their version of events, consider and hear about the impact of their actions and the actions of others, and problem-solve the best way to move forward with the relationship. These conversations can sometimes be difficult, and it takes a lot of courage to have them. However, with a supportive and consistent structure in place, this stage allows us to engage in difficult conversations together in a positive and constructive manner.

The restore stage is explored in detail in Chapter 6.

 Toolkit: Dealing with student resistance

What I have detailed so far in this chapter is a way to enact a behaviour education approach in your classroom through a whole-school staged response model. I've provided a few examples that illustrate how things might play out. However, I am cognisant that, in many classrooms, teachers and students won't always move smoothly through the stages as detailed in the examples given. As a teacher, you are likely to encounter resistance and argumentation from students.

First and foremost, it is normal for young people to want to test the boundaries. Encountering resistance is your opportunity to adopt an educative approach in your practice. It is important that you remain calm in the face of resistance and argumentation, and continue to show care and empathy towards students. This is a skill that is tough to learn, and it may not come naturally to you, but if you are able to stay calm and present you have the ability to de-escalate the situation and move seamlessly through the stages.

Staying calm in heated moments is one of the greatest skills a person can possess. It enables you to think rationally and clearly. One of the greatest lessons I learnt in my time as a Constable for Victoria Police was how to stay calm amid someone else's chaos. It reminds me of a very famous saying: when their storm meets our calm, co-regulation occurs.

The All Blacks rugby union team has a mantra to 'keep a blue head' amid times of stress and uncertainty. Basically, keeping a blue head means controlling your attention, focusing on being in the moment, clear, loose and expressive. Staying in the blue-head zone allows you to problem-solve and assist others with whatever situation has arisen, whether that be out on the rugby field or in the classroom. The All Blacks believe games are won when leaders keep a blue head. The opposite, keeping a red head, sees a person anxious, focused only on the result they want, aggressive and inhibited. Not much gets done or achieved in this zone. Do what you need to do to stay in the blue-head zone – box breathing, visualisation of something blue and so on.

When you are calm and in the blue-head zone, you can then focus on using dialogue with students to correct behaviour. As part of this approach, I suggest four strategies to shift the focus of the conversation and to de-escalate it. These four strategies, which are amalgamations of my learnings as a Constable for Victoria Police and as a school leader in student management roles, are explained next.

Divert and dilute

The divert and dilute strategy is an add-on to the AID technique. First, it is important that you clearly detail the off-task behaviour that is occurring and the impact that it is having on others. This raises the student's behavioural awareness and provides a justifiable reason as to why the conversation is occurring. After raising the student's behavioural awareness, you then direct them towards what needs to happen to bring them back on-task with their learning. Often this is all that is needed. However, at the end of the do/do differently statement you might also encounter argumentation from students, which almost always draws you into a dispute together with the student. This is what you want to avoid. The divert and dilute strategy allows you to do this by shifting the focus of the conversation and then diluting it. The two phases are described below:

1. **Divert argumentation:** if argumentation ensues you need to divert the focus of the conversation and avoid being drawn into a dispute. You can use diversion words and phrases such as 'even so', 'regardless', 'in any case', 'that's not the concern here', and 'at the moment that is not important'. If you have read the work of Dr Bill Rogers, an Australian behaviour management specialist, you will see that diversion statements are similar to what he calls reaching 'partial agreement' (see Rogers, 2007, 2015) with a student to escape behavioural debates.

2. **Dilute response:** once you have diverted the focus of the argument, you dilute the student's response by reiterating the core concern or required action.

The divert and dilute strategy sees you being firm, fair and focused in your response to resistance and argumentation. Let's take a look at some examples of the strategy in use.

Example 1

> **Teacher:** 'Michael, we're currently engaging in silent reading and you are talking to James behind you [action]. This is impacting the ability of other students to focus on reading [impact]. I need you to stop talking and to focus on reading silently [do/do differently].'
>
> **Michael:** 'Oh, come on, sir, Johnny is talking and you haven't said anything to him! Why haven't you pulled him up on that?'

If you respond with, 'Johnny isn't talking!', this is likely to escalate the situation. Instead you could respond with:

> 'Even so, Michael, I am asking you to not talk during this activity [divert]. Thank you for focusing back on the learning task [dilute].'

Or:

> 'That might be the case. At the moment, though, I need you to turn and face the front of the classroom and start reading [divert]. Thank you for turning around and giving your full attention to the book in front of you [dilute].'

Example 2

> **Teacher:** 'Janine, you haven't started writing yet [action]. Not starting will mean that you won't have feedback in which to build upon your essay in the next lesson [impact]. I need you to pick up a pen and make a start on your draft plan or introduction [do/do differently].'
>
> **Janine:** 'But I have my pen out on my desk! It's right there! Look!'

If you respond with, 'That isn't your pen. It is Lisa's!', this is likely to escalate the situation. Instead you could respond with:

> 'The concern isn't whether your pen is out, Janine. The concern is commencing the writing task [divert]. Thank you for making a start with your work [dilute].'

Or:

> 'Even so, I need you to start the writing task [divert]. Thank you for picking up a pen and making a start with your work [dilute].'

At the end of the dilute statement there is space given to provide a 'thank you' to the student. This pre-emptive gesture closes the loop on the conversation with the student and acknowledges the change in behaviour before it has occurred. It signals to the student that you are appreciative of their change efforts. It's delivered in a positive manner, which also reinforces the on-task behaviour that needs to occur. The divert and dilute strategy is powerful in the sense that it counteracts the need to slip into self-defense mode when we are challenged in an argument. Rogers (2007, 2015) argued that partial agreement, which occurs as part of the divert phase, is a useful way to block tangent arguments from dominating the interaction. It is a way in which to sidestep an argument and redirect the student to focus exclusively on what you want/need them to do to get back on task with their learning. One of the strengths of adopting an educative approach to behaviour management is acknowledging that, as teachers, we are not in the business of 'winning' arguments with students. We are there to assist them with their learning, and the best way to do that is to avoid the trap of argumentation entirely.

Dix (2017) explained that it is important for teachers to have microscripts ready to enact when we encounter student resistance to reasonable instructions. The divert and dilute strategy, while seeming naturally embedded in dialogue with students, requires much practice in order to feel comfortable enacting it. One way to do this is to engage in the role-play activities detailed at the end of this chapter and, as part of this, ask the person with you to engage in some resistance so that you can practise your divert and dilute strategy. Play around with three to four key phrases in these role-plays so that you can transfer them to the classroom as part of your behaviour education practice.

Chilli burger

I learnt this conflict resolution strategy as a Constable with Victoria Police. It is good to use when students are resisting activities they need to do. For example, you might have distributed a task in which students need to research a current world issue, but you catch a student playing games on their laptop instead. When you approach the student, they express a strong desire to continue playing. It is important at this stage not to jump straight to the spicy chilli – 'I'll take your laptop then!'. First, you need to give the student the bun, some margarine and perhaps some lettuce. Depending upon your school context, you may need many more supportive layers. Then, when you get to the middle of your burger, you reach the chilli. The chilli is a statement that is delivered more directly, but respectfully, and includes information on what will happen next if the off-task behaviour continues.

Here is an examples of the chilli burger strategy in use.

> **Teacher:** 'Jack, I can see you are playing a game on your laptop [action], which is distracting you from the learning task [impact]. I need you to stop and focus on the research learning task we are all doing in class today [do/do differently]. Do you need help with this? [offer of assistance]'
>
> **Jack:** 'But I really just want to play this game!'
>
> **Burger bun:** 'I understand that, Jack [acknowledgement of student]. But now is not the time to be playing games on your laptop [action]. I need you to continue on with the research task as requested [do/do differently]'
>
> **Jack:** 'This game is fun and I am almost finished the stage'

Margarine: 'I am sure it is, Jack [acknowledgement of student]. Now isn't the time to play games but you will have time to play the game in your own time outside of class [action]. Right now, in this lesson together, I need you to close the game and start with the task please [do/do differently].'

Jack: 'I can't! Can't you just wait?!'

Chilli: 'Jack, I have now asked a couple of times and it seems to be challenging for you at the moment to listen to a reasonable instruction [acknowledgement of situation]. I need you to close down the game and refocus on the learning task [action]. The next time we speak about this same issue I will be storing your laptop at the front of the classroom and I will provide you alternate work to help you engage with the task [the chilli]. Thank you for your cooperation with me here, Jack [pre-emptive acknowledgement of changed behaviour].'

Once you reach the chilli, and you tell the student what will happen next if the same off-task behaviour occurs again, it is important that you follow through with your next-step actions. When there is no follow-through, the chilli becomes a hollow statement with no influence (it loses its heat).

Choice funnelling

This strategy is about allowing students to choose how they behave and to experience the natural consequences that follow. Sometimes we need to provide students with a choice of two options and allow them the time and space to choose which avenue they would like to go down. Of course, the two choices can both be things that we would like them to do (e.g. 'move here' or 'move there'), but the illusion of choice is there nonetheless. It is a classic behavioural technique that has been used in parenting, policing, schools and other organisations for many years. It is a good way to highlight to the students that they have ownership of their behaviour while also clarifying what the available choices are.

I have often opted to use choice funnelling as a first port of call when I encounter 'spot fires' in the classroom such as a mobile phone being used, a basketball being thrown around and so on. Choice funnelling can also be used in combination with the divert and dilute strategy and the chilli burger strategy, especially when a direction has been, or continues to be, ignored. It may also form part of your dialogical approach with students when moving through the first four stages of the 5 Rs.

In his seminal texts on behaviour management, Bill Rogers (2007, 2015) wrote about the concept of 'forced choices', which sees a teacher present a student with two choices: one being the desired behavioural outcome and the other being a natural consequence of refusing a reasonable instruction. The key to a successful choice funnelling is in the use of the keyword 'or' and, importantly, the associated follow-up by the teacher.

Rogers (2007, 2015) argued that it is best to start with small consequences first and ensure that those consequences are things that can be realistically followed through on. They cannot be large, grandiose consequences that do not match the student's actions and, equally, they cannot be things that go unchecked.

Let's take a look at some examples of choice funnelling.

Example 1: Moving through the 5 Rs

A teacher, Amira, has used the AID technique to remind (Stage 1) and restate (Stage 2) with her student Anne, in relation to a need to work quietly during that part of the lesson. Very soon after Amira walks away, Anne starts chatting again quite loudly. Amira uses choice funnelling to alert Anne to the fact that she is about to be repositioned in the classroom: 'Anne, you can choose to work silently, or be repositioned to another spot in the classroom.'

Example 2: Spot fire

Luke pulls out a tennis ball and starts bouncing it on his desk. This is the first time that the teacher, Sally, has spoken to Luke. She says: 'Luke, you can put that ball back in your bag, or you can leave it on my desk. Your choice.'

Sometimes, the choices aligned with natural consequences may need to be more serious, such as calling home.

De-personalisation through positive affirmations

This strategy is good to use when students turn your reasonable requests into personalised attacks. It is a way in which to challenge the student's underlying assumptions about how you see them as a learner and person.

A central component of high-growth relationships is ensuring students know that we care deeply about them and their learning. Explicitly correcting assumptions that suggest otherwise may, in the first instance, allow for the argument and resistance to disperse immediately. It is a strategy that sees you use a positive affirmation about the student's character and disposition to show them your request has nothing to do with them as a person; rather, that you have high expectations for their learning. Let's return to Jack as an example.

Teacher: 'Jack, I can see you are playing a game on your laptop [action], which is distracting you from the learning task [impact]. I need you to stop and focus on the research learning task we are all doing in class today [do/do differently]. Do you need help with this? [offer of assistance]'

> **Jack:** 'Come on! You're always on my back. You hate me!'
>
> **Teacher:** 'Jack, you are a valued member of this classroom and I recognise your strengths, notably your perseverance and determination with learning [positive affirmation]. My request is related to your actions in this moment, and not who I think you are as a person [divert the belief of a personalised attack]. You are playing a game on your laptop [action] which is distracting you from the learning task we are doing [impact]. I need you to stop playing the game so you can focus back on the learning task [do/do differently]. Thank you for closing your laptop and reconnecting to the task, Jack [pre-emptive acknowledgement of changed behaviour].'

The three strategies to deal with resistance and argumentation that I have detailed here are by no means exhaustive, and there are many more. They are, however, three strong strategies that you can add to your behaviour education toolkit. Practising these three strategies in *role-play activities* with colleagues will allow you to feel more confident in your ability to enact them and respond to students who need a bit more support.

CHAPTER SUMMARY AND REFLECTION

In this chapter I outlined a whole-school approach to behaviour education through my 5 Rs whole-school behaviour education model. We discussed the first four stages – remind, restate, reposition and relocate – and how these can be used to respond to students' off-task behaviours in the classroom. I also discussed hinting techniques that allow students to self-correct before the various stages of the model are enacted. I concluded by discussing four strategies that teachers can employ to deal with resistance and argumentation.

You can expand upon your learning and understanding by engaging in role-play activities with colleagues. Role-plays improve your confidence with enacting behaviour education strategies, and they promote better performance with redirection conversations and dealing with resistance. They also help you to develop strong problem-solving skills while seeking feedback from mentors as to how they might approach a given scenario. I have included four role-play situations that you can enact as part of a behaviour education learning team. They allow you to think more deeply about how you might put the different stages of the model into practice.

- **Scenario 1:** You have your students sitting in the Mini Us set-up. At one table, Mark is pestering one of the other students (e.g., taking pens, moving students' paper around). You have warned Mark to stop but he is persisting with the behaviour. What do you do?

- **Scenario 2:** Susan keeps talking to the student next to her, Sam, while you are trying to present material at the front of the class. What do you do?

- **Scenario 3:** You are asking your class questions to help them understand a key concept in the lesson you are teaching. Lucas is raising his hand and offering frivolous answers in an attempt to get a laugh from the two students next to him. What do you do?

* Add resistance to this role-play

- **Scenario 4:** You see Robert drawing in his book and not undertaking the task that he is supposed to be doing. He isn't distracting any other students but he is refusing to engage in the lesson. What do you do?

    * Add resistance to this role-play

CHAPTER 6

RESTORATIVE PRACTICES

'It is in the shelter of each other that the people live.'
– Irish proverb

Like the philosophy of Ubuntu that we touched on in Part I, the concept of restorative practices is a whole-school teaching and learning approach that encourages supportive, respectful and peaceful behaviour. Restorative practices build and maintain positive relationships. German theoretical physicist Albert Einstein once said, 'Peace cannot be kept by force; it can only be achieved by understanding.' There is no better way to think about the purpose of restorative practices. Restorative practices, especially restorative justice conference conversations, are a way to leverage the power of dialogue with one another to understand the causes and consequences of our actions. It is through this understanding that we learn how to be better people, for ourselves and for the world around us. Therein lies an essential consideration for the purpose of schools. We owe it to ourselves to not only assist students to be the best learners they can be, but also the best people they can be. Through restorative practices we can assist students in gaining a better understanding of themselves and how they operate in this world. I believe this to be truly one of the greatest gifts we can give students.

This chapter comprises Stage 5 (restore) in my 5 Rs whole-school behaviour education model, which I detailed in Chapter 5 (Figure 5.1).

I'll start the chapter by discussing the differences between restorative justice and retributive justice. Next, I'll explain how to set the scene for a restorative justice conference conversation, including considerations for the physical space and the inclusion of sensory support measures. I'll conclude with a script that you can use to facilitate restorative justice conference conversations.

Chapter learning intentions

By the end of this chapter, you will be able to:

- adopt a restorative justice approach over a retributive approach
- plan for and set up a restorative justice conference conversation
- use a script to facilitate a restorative justice conference conversation.

A shifting tide in schools

In the introduction to this book I pronounced that managing bodies in and through school like an assembly line is no longer appropriate given the current epoch we are in. There is a long history of using discipline in schools to punish students for doing the wrong thing. The thinking in the past was that such measures would 'bring children into line', and that retribution was needed to produce a society of hard workers (and consumers of authority). This approach is known as retributive justice. As we developed a more sophisticated understanding of behaviour management in schools during the late 1980s and early 1990s, a movement towards restorative justice emerged. Table 6.1 compares and contrasts these two approaches.

Table 6.1: Retributive versus restorative justice in schools

	Retributive justice	Restorative justice
Focus	The act is a wrongdoing against the law/rules.	The act is a wrongdoing against the people and their relationships.
Fault	The fault rests on the individual who committed the wrongdoing.	The fault shifts from the person to the duty, commitment and responsibilities between people.
Ensuing action	A punishment must be imposed in proportion to the wrongdoing that was committed.	Agreed-upon actions are enacted to repair the harm between people, which might be physical, emotional and/or psychological.
What this looks like in schools	Monotonous tasks such as writing of lines Isolation Detention Suspension Belittling, sarcasm, name-calling Removal of privileges	Relational problem-solving Teachers and students working together Solution-focused actions Repairing harm

There exists a large body of evidence that has demonstrated that a retributive approach in schools does not contribute to the creation of a positive learning environment (Cruz & Rodl, 2018; Mielke & Farrington, 2021) and is, in fact detrimental to students' learning and wellbeing (Mowen et al., 2020), especially for students from marginalised or disadvantaged backgrounds (Hoffmann, 2016). Simply put, reliance on retributive practices to correct student behaviour in schools is inappropriate. Restorative practices, though, are appropriate as they are inherently educational and focused on repairing relationships so that positive learning environments are maintained. They are essential for leading positive classrooms.

Restorative practices in schools are generally focused on facilitating a conference between a teacher and a student, or group of students, to address a specific incident and to rebuild the relationships that have been harmed. However, simply labelling a conference as a 'restorative practice' is not enough. Research has shown that many schools purport to espouse restorative practices, but in practice the conferences are used to exercise control and reinforce the need for the student to 'do' or 'not do' something or to 'be' or 'not be' a type of person in the classroom. This cannot be considered to be a restorative practice. In her comparative case study of restorative practices in two schools, one in Canada and one in Scotland, Reimer (2019) concluded that:

> Restorative justice is used in the service of whatever the predominant relational objectives are in each unique school. In a school where relational objectives are of social control – focused on compliance, rules, behaviour, and punishment – restorative justice is utilized to strengthen that control. In a school where the objective is of social engagement – focused on relationships of equality and mutuality, with a focus on empowerment and growth – restorative justice is utilized to strengthen that engagement.

The problem arises when schools espouse the enactment of practices under the umbrella of a restorative justice philosophy, but the teachers and school leaders have insufficient skills or knowledge of restorative justice to ensure that those practices are being enacted properly. In the absence of proper professional learning, teachers and school leaders can find themselves demanding an apology from students, or jumping straight to labelling their behaviour as inappropriate without allowing the student the opportunity to think deeply about the cause of and reasoning for their actions. As a result, the student might not connect with the restorative process or think critically about their actions and the harm that has been caused. Instead, they may sit there and play along with whatever is being said, agreeing so that they can get out of the conversation quickly. The teacher or school leader may think the conversation was a success because the student sat there nodding in agreeance, but the fact is, they lost the student the moment they demanded an apology or labelled the student without giving them an opportunity to speak. In the very next lesson, the behaviour continues and we are stuck in a loop of compounded behavioural concerns in the classroom.

I use the term 'restorative practices' in a way that strengthens the creation and maintenance of high-growth relationships between teachers and students. It is, in Reimer's (2019) sentiment, a way to empower students and enhance their personal growth. The teacher and the student work together to repair harm and co-construct positive ways to move forward. I believe restorative practices to be dialogical; that is, it is not a one-way street. It is a process of engaging in dialogue with students to better understand them and their actions, and to encourage the student to think more deeply about what happened and how to move forward positively.

When teachers adopt a restorative mindset over a retributive mindset they support students to accept responsibility and take accountability for their actions, and reflect on the impact their actions have on others. Importantly, they create the space needed to educate students on how to repair relationships and build new skills in doing so. It is an approach that considers students as important contributors to the success of the whole school community. The reflective conversations that occur better prepare students for the behaviour change that contributes to positive learning environments. The teacher *leads* student behaviour through restorative practices rather than seeking to *control* student behaviour through retributive practices.

The following six principles reflect the values and concepts for implementing restorative practices in schools. These principles act as guiding beacons for teachers and school leaders to adhere to, while simultaneously acting as check measures to ensure that the school has indeed adopted restorative practices as part of their overall behaviour education approach.

The principles are as follows:

1. Restorative practices acknowledge that building and maintaining positive relationships is central to the success of the whole school community.

2. Restorative practices are enacted in ways that address students' off-task behaviours and harm while strengthening relationships.
3. Restorative practices focus on the harm caused rather than only on the breaking of rules and laws, and do not bring into question a person's moral character.
4. Restorative practices promote collaborative problem-solving in relation to the identified harm.
5. Restorative practices empower students to change their behaviour and to focus on building social and emotional skills.
6. Restorative practices enhance students' sense of responsibility.

If your school has adopted a staged response model to behaviour education, such as my 5 Rs whole-school behaviour education model (Figure 5.1), a restorative practice that will likely occur is a restorative justice conference conversation between the teacher and the student after Stage 4 (relocation) has been reached. The next sections consider how to facilitate a restorative justice conference conversation.

Setting the scene for a restorative justice conference conversation

Before a restorative justice conversation can be had between a teacher and a student, there needs to be time and space available in which to do so. As mentioned in Chapter 5, this is an *enabling school structure* that supports a whole-school approach to behaviour education. Each school will do this differently and it will depend on teachers' schedules and timetables.

A restorative justice conversation usually focuses on one isolated incident in the classroom that led to damage to relationships. An individual conference should last for no more than 20 to 30 minutes, and a community conference (between a teacher and a group of students) for no more than 40 to 60 minutes. The teacher, in consultation with the year level coordinator, principal or assistant principal, might organise to meet the student(s) at the start of lunchtime; or, in consultation with parents, directly after school on the day of the relocation. Ideally, a restorative justice conference conversation shouldn't occur during other lessons in the school day, as this detracts from students' learning in that class. It is important, though, to ensure that the restorative justice conference conversation occurs as close to the incident as possible, ideally within two days of the incident. It is no use having a restorative justice conference conversation four weeks after the incident, as chances are both the teacher and the student have forgotten what has happened, and the student may be unable to think deeply about the harm that was caused because of the time passed.

You should also consider the space where the restorative justice conference conversation will be held. It needs to be a space that is comfortable, private and free from distraction. In the past I have often held them in the wellbeing offices, or the more private offices in the administration part of the school building. If a classroom has to be used, I implore you to use a classroom that is out of the view of other students. The space also needs to be a non-intimidating space where the student and teacher can sit and have a dialogical conversation together. If there are couches in the room, that is great – make use of them. Even though it is a formal conversation and designed to extract deep thought about actions and consequences, it is better if students feel comfortable enough to do so. The environment they're in plays a big part in this. Remember, one of the principles of the conversation is to empower students' sense of responsibility, and this is best achieved in environments where they feel safe, secure and comfortable. It is a talking *with* and not a talking *to*.

You should also consider whether it will be an individual conference between a teacher and a single student, or whether it will be a community conference between a teacher and a group of students, or between students. Depending upon the situation that has occurred, you will need to think about where the students sit in relation to one another. If it is a community conference between two students who have pushed and shoved each other in class, it is probably not a good idea to seat them in close proximity to each other unless you can be reasonably sure that no further altercation will occur in the conference. If you are not sure, it is best to exercise caution and have an additional staff member join you – likely to be a member of school leadership – so that they can sit between the two students during the conference.

In my own practice, I have generally set the conference up as depicted in Figure 6.1. I have positioned students in a semicircle around myself and a portable whiteboard. I have used the whiteboard to make notes and jot down keywords the students say. I have also used the board to draw students' attention to the three pillars of CBT– thoughts, feelings and behaviour – to enhance their ability to see connections between their thoughts and their actions.

Figure 6.1: Setting the scence for a restorative justice conversation

It is a good idea to bring your sensory box (Chapter 3) to the restorative justice conference conversation. This will allow students to self-regulate during the conversation if they feel stressed and uncertain. This sensory integration allows a sense of mindfulness to enter the conversation and, if the student feels the need to, they can de-escalate themselves via different tactile items. I have experienced much success bringing the sensory box along to restorative justice conference conversations, namely because we cannot reasonably expect students to sit there like adults and engage in eye contact for the entire 20 to 60 minutes while simultaneously having a deep conversation about behavioural cause and effect. As adults, even we struggle to do this sometimes. We must recognise the limitations of human development and, in some instances, the effects of trauma. If the student is happily talking and reflecting while squeezing a stress ball or playing with playdough, that is great. You are still achieving the same outcome, and you are assisting the student through the process using sensory supports.

Toolkit: Facilitating a restorative justice conference conversation

With the time for the restorative justice conference conversation set and a comfortable space to meet, it is now time to discuss how to facilitate the conversation.

A restorative justice conference conversation has two purposes:

1. **rebuild** trust
2. **restart** with agreed-upon actions.

To do this requires the facilitator to make use of affective questioning. Affective questioning promotes critical reflection which elicits empathy, remorse and, most importantly, learning. When using affective questioning it is important to:

- ask questions that encourage the students to engage in self-reflection
- build upon the student or students' answers so that they are able to engage in solution-focused thinking. However, also understand that in some instances there might not be an immediate solution present and you might require further conversations.
- be empathetic and understanding of students' viewpoints. It is important not to undermine their viewpoints from a position of power.

- enact empathetic listening (Chapter 1). This requires *listening for understanding* rather than *listening to respond*. Allow students the space to provide a narrative of their version of events without interuption. If there are multiple students in the conference, it is important that a common understanding of empathetic listening and everyone having an equal opportunity to be heard is understood as a required norm before the conference starts.
- look for opportunities to validate students' feelings with concrete statements such as, 'I can see that retelling this story has made you upset' or 'I can see that you are feeling frustrated.'
- avoid making judgements about the students or commenting on their moral character.

The structure of the affective questioning will vary depending upon the context and focus of the restorative justice conference. However, a good starting point is to explain the purpose of the conference, establish agreed-upon norms and explain how the conference will unfold. You might start the conversation using the following script:

> Thank you [individual student or group of students] for coming along today to [this restorative justice conversation or community conference]. I appreciate your time and effort in ensuring we can move forward positively with our relationship and our learning in class. The purpose of today is to acknowledge the harm that has been caused between us, and to figure out ways to repair the harm and to move forward positively.
>
> Before we start, and before I explain how this conference will work, we need to establish some agreed-upon norms. Norms are shared standards of behaviour, and they are there so that everyone can have a common understanding of how we can participate successfully in dialogue with one another. There are five norms today. They are:
>
> 1. We listen to each other and we don't interrupt when someone is speaking.
> 2. We take turns and we share airtime equally among ourselves.
> 3. We share our own ideas, and we explain them as best we can.
> 4. We respect each other's ideas, even if we believe them to be wrong or they are different to ours.

5. We respectfully disagree, which means we don't always have to agree but we are open to seeing other views.

Do I need to explain any of these norms further? Do you understand fully what they mean? Are there any that I have missed or that we need to add?

Okay, great. It sounds like we all understand the norms associated with today's conversation together. I will now explain how the conference will work.

Individual conference

You will have the opportunity to tell your side of the story. Once you have finished, I might ask you some questions to get some more information. Once we have fully explored your version of events, I will talk about mine. You will then have the opportunity to ask me some questions, too. Once both our stories have been told, we will explore the harm together. We will work together to repair the harm and to come up with positive ways to move forward with our relationship. Are there any questions that you would like to ask before we start?

Community conference

You will each have the opportunity to tell your side of the story. Once you have finished, I might ask you some questions to get some more information. Once we have fully explored your version of events, the next student will tell their side of the story. Once again, I may ask some questions. I will then tell my side of the story. Once I have finished, you will have the opportunity to ask me some questions or ask the other students some questions, respectfully. Once we have fully explored our respective versions of events, we will explore the harm together. We will work together to repair the harm and to come up with positive ways to move forward with our relationships. Are there any questions that you would like to ask before we start?

With agreed-upon norms in place, and with students understanding the purpose of the conference and how it will unfold, you can then move on to the dialogical conversation. If you are not yet comfortable doing this organically, and as a means for professional learning, I have included a script that you can use in practice and with other teachers in role-play scenarios. Having a script for guidance reduces the risk that the conversation will go off topic and wander into realms where it shouldn't. A script also ensures that if the conversation does go off track, you can redirect yourself or students back to the questions that need to be explored.

The following script is adapted from Thorsborne and Vinegrad's (2004) work on restorative practices in classrooms. It is a brief, structured set of questions that are designed to elucidate critical thinking and to de-escalate a situation so that a positive outcome can ensue. There are five steps in the questions: tell the story, explore the harm, repair the harm, reach an agreement, and summary and follow-up.

Step 1: Tell the story

This step establishes what happened in the situation and seeks to identify the causes of the behaviour. The questions are:

- In your own words, can you tell me your version of what happened?
- What were you thinking when the situation happened?
- How did that make you feel?
- What were the intended outcomes of your behaviour? [Purpose of behaviour.]
- Is it okay to do that? Why or why not? [Critique the purpose of behaviour.]
- What are the expectations in our classroom and school about [the behaviour]?
- Did your behaviour align with that expectation?
- What could you have done differently in the situation? [Alternative options.]
- Who could help support you with that different approach? [Additional support for alternative.]

Step 2: Explore the harm

This step is about exploring the harm and who has been affected by what happened. This part of the conference aims to develop students' empathy towards others, as well as their ability to see the connection between their behaviour and the harm caused. It is not an opportunity to be punitive or pass judgement on the student, e.g. 'you did this, you are bad, and now you will be punished'. Nor is it space for the adult to do all the talking. Indeed, much of the learning for the student will come from the support and guidance from the adult through skills in prompting and questioning.

The questions are:

- Who has been affected by the behaviour that you enacted in this situation? In what ways?
- What do you think they must have thought and felt? How do you know?

For those who have been harmed, the questions are:

- How did the situation make you feel?
- How have you been harmed or affected?
- What would you like to see happen to make the situation better for you?

Step 3: Repair the harm

This step seeks to ascertain what needs to happen so that everyone can move forward positively. It connects the person harmed to the person who has caused the harm and allows problem-solving dialogue to enter the conference so that the harm is repaired and doesn't occur again. If students are not willing to consider ways to repair the harm, it may be necessary to establish firm and fair boundaries to protect everyone from further harm, while also establishing a need to come together again to discuss the solutions to the issue further.

If the conversation is between two students, I have often started this part of the conference by getting both students to acknowledge one thing they admire about the other person or one strength they see. I remind students that there's no expectation that we like everyone we work with, but we *are* expected to be kind regardless. For example, a student might say, 'I acknowledge that Andrew is really good at sport and I admire his passion for football.' This is a really positive way to start to repair the harm between students and sets an optimistic scene for what needs to happen to repair and move forward.

The subsequent questions are:

- What do you think needs to happen so that we can all move forward positively together?
- What do you think [other student] might need to hear from you in order to move forward positively?
- What else could you do to fix the problem with [person]?
- Is there anything else that could be done?

For those who have been harmed, the questions are:

- Does [other student's] response seem like a fair and reasonable way to move forward together positively?
- Is there anything else that you would like to add?

An apology might surface during this stage, but it is important that you do not force this from a position of authoritative power. Students might not apologise because they haven't developed the skills do so, even if they want to and acknowledge that they should. In this case, the teacher should explicitly teach students what to do and what not to do when making an apology. This might include the teacher providing worked examples and sentence stems, such as:

> I apologise [name] for [behaviour]. Moving forward I [change].
>
> I can see that I made you feel [feeling] by [behaviour] and I am sorry. Next time I will [change].

A good apology has four facets:

1. The student identifies what they did wrong.
2. The student states why it was wrong or the harm it has caused.
3. The student details what they will do differently in the future.
4. The student expresses care towards those who have been harmed.

You may need to explicitly teach students that when making an authentic apology they shouldn't:

- make an excuse, such as 'I was just bored'
- blame someone else for their behaviour
- expect forgiveness to be granted straight away (there might be a process of healing needed).

Step 4: Reach an agreement

This step sees participants working together to co-construct an agreement on ways in which to move forward positively with the relationship. This might be an agreement on more positive ways to deal with the situation if it were to arise again, such as seeking help from the teacher in the first instance. The questions are:

- If this situation happens again, what can we do differently to ensure a more positive outcome?
- What will the plan be moving forward?

Step 5: Summary and follow-up

This step sees the facilitator summarise the discussion of the conference so that everyone is on the same page with what has been said and agreed. A plan for follow-up is constructed so everyone can ascertain if they are adhering to the agreed-upon actions that have stemmed from the conference.

First, provide a summary of the conference and ask everyone how they are feeling; then ask the following questions:

- What will happen if our agreed-upon actions aren't followed?
- When would be a good time for us to come together again to have a five-minute conversation to see if we are adhering to what we have discussed?

You then finish the conference by thanking everyone for their time. You might also provide positive feedback relating to how well the students spoke, how they explored the situation and how they came together to problem-solve. Tying off a conversation with a positive primer such as this is a great way to end the conference.

CHAPTER SUMMARY AND REFLECTION

In this chapter I discussed Stage 5 of the 5 Rs whole-school behaviour education model: restorative practices. I explored the differences between retributive justice and restorative justice, expressing the need to adopt the latter in schools as we continually develop and maintain high-growth relationships. I provided recommendations for how to set up restorative justice conferences, both individual and community. I argued that the facilitation of these conferences is dependent upon enabling school structures. I concluded the chapter with a script that you can use when facilitating restorative justice conference conversations, focusing the dialogue on acknowledging the harm and the ways in which to repair it to move forward positively.

Take a moment now to reflect on your learning and understanding through the *circle of action* thinking tool, which is best used in dialogue with a mentor or critical friend. It will help you engage in concept mapping, affording you the opportunity to think more deeply about how restorative practices can be embedded in your individual classrooms, different year levels and your school more broadly.

- How can [I/we] best embed restorative practices in:
    - One of my specific classes?
    - Across all of my classes?
    - Across all of the school's classes in a specific year level?
    - Across all of the school's classes at a whole-school level?
    - In my inner circle (of friends, family, the people I know)?
    - In my community (my school, my neighbourhood)?
    - In the world (beyond my immediate environment)?
- What do [I/we] need to further enhance [my/our] capacity and skills to facilitate a restorative justice conference in the above situations?

CONCLUSION

STATEMENT OF ACTION

'The journey of a thousand miles begins with a single step.'
– Lao Tzu

When I considered how best to close this book out, I decided against simply providing a summary of the chapters herein. First, I didn't see much value in doing so. The chapters are there to revisit and simply summarising them does not serve the intended purpose of this book: to provide a case for change. Second, I thought to myself, if I were a teacher reading this book, what would *I* want at the end of this book? The answer was not a summary. It was the opportunity to develop a statement of action. As a teacher, I would want the invitation and space to be able to think deeply about everything I had just read, so I could make a solid commitment to myself and my practice as an educator. What are my key learnings from this book? What will I do now? What are my next steps? And so, in review of the whole topic of behaviour education, I cannot close this book out without affording you the opportunity to write a statement of action. This statement will be what you commit to doing moving forward to better the lives of your students or the professional practice of the teachers you work with.

Before we get to that, though, we must first take stock of where we have been on this journey together. Let's do this through one of Aesop's fables, *The Bundle of Sticks*:

> An old man had four quarrelsome sons who were constantly working against one another. As a result, there was no peace in the house. To educate his four sons on the importance of togetherness, he asked one of his sons to bring a bundle of four sticks wrapped together with twine. To his eldest son, he remarked, 'I want you to try and break the bundle.' The son strained and strained, but with all his efforts was unable to break the bundle. Each of the remaining three sons then tried to break the bundle but none of them were successful. The father then asked the youngest son to untie the bundle. Each of the four sons were then handed a single stick and were asked to break it, with each son easily able to do so. 'Do you see my meaning?' said their father. 'Individually, you are vulnerable, but together, you are strong. In unity is strength.'

The central message of Aesop's fable is that we are stronger when we are together. It is for this reason that I used the analogy of a geodesic dome in the first chapter of this book. Behaviour education is not something we do separately from others – it is not an act of individualism. It is, essentially, a theorem of togetherness. It's a sense of Ubuntu whereby we realise that we are because everyone else is. Schools are stronger, safer and more enjoyable when there is a geodesic dome built around each student who enters the school gates. It is a non-punitive way of addressing students' off-task behaviours and educating them on ways in which to better connect with their learning and other people. The sticks stay strong when they are bundled together.

My closing message to you is this: leverage what has been written in this book to bring the sticks together in your school. Changing mindsets from behaviour management to behaviour education takes time, but you might just be the twine in Aesop's fable that brings everyone in your school together, onto the same page.

In the introduction of this book, you were given a blank box in which you were given the space to reflect on your own behaviour education practice. You might now take the opportunity to revisit that page.

What do you notice? What has changed? What has stayed the same? What impact have the words in this book had? Why? There is power in doing this because it shows just how far you have now come with your confidence, knowledge and desire to investigate certain topics further. You might like to take the time to document these changes in the box below.

It is at this point that I congratulate you. It takes courage, determination and passion to pick up a book on a topic related to your profession with the view of enhancing your own practice so that you can better connect with students and lead positive classrooms. I have no doubt that your students will benefit immensely from the behaviour education practices that you enact in your classroom moving forward. However, we cannot end there. Even though you and I are about to part ways, there is still much to do and so much more to learn. I now invite you to write a statement of action regarding the next steps for your behaviour education practice or the behaviour education practice in your school. A statement of action is a commitment that you make to perform, or work towards achieving, a desired action/outcome. It is an action-focused statement that connects back to something you thought about in Chapter 1 of this book: – your *why* in education.

Here's an example for you to consider.

> **My why**
>
> To support young people to become confident, creative, critical thinkers who value supporting others in the name of positive social transformation.
>
> **Statement of action**
>
> With the knowledge that I have obtained through reading this book, I will provide professional learning to the three staff within my faculty on how to build high-growth relationships with students. I will advocate that in two of our whole-school staff meetings this year, we are provided the opportunity to practise restorative justice conference conversations with other teachers. These two actionable steps will enhance the collective capacity of my school to support students to become confident, creative, critical thinkers who value their relationships with others.

With your statement of action now documented, I wish you well on the rest of your behaviour education journey. From the bottom of my heart, thank you for reading and connecting with me through the words I've written on these pages.

REFERENCES

Allen, K.A., Grove, C., Berger, E., Marinucci, A., & Warton, W. (2022). *High impact wellbeing strategies*. Department of Education Victoria. Accessed 12 January 2024. www.education.vic.gov.au/Documents/school/teachers/teachingresources/practice/High_Impact_Wellbeing_Strategies.pdf

Apple, M. (2004). *Ideology and Curriculum* (3rd ed). RoutledgeFalmer.

Australian Institute for Teaching and School Leadership (AITSL). (2017). *Australian professional standards for teachers*. Accessed 12 January 2024. www.aitsl.edu.au/teach/standards

Baker, P.H. (2005). Managing Student Behavior: How Ready are Teachers to Meet the Challenge? *American Secondary Education, 33*(3), 51-64.

Bambara, L.M, Janney, R., & Snell, M.E. (2015). *Behaviour support* (3rd ed). Brookes Publishing Co.

Barker, K., Poed, S., & Whitefield, P. (2022). *School-wide positive behaviour support: The Australian handbook* (1st ed.). Taylor & Francis.

Brackett, M. (2019). Permission to feel: *Unlock the power of emotions to help yourself and your child thrive*. Quercus Books.

Bronfenbrenner, U. (1977). Toward an experimental ecology of human development. *American Psychologist, 32*(7), 513-531.

Bronfenbrenner, U. (1979). *The ecology of human development: Experiments by nature and design*. Harvard University Press.

Bronfenbrenner, U. (1993). The ecology of cognitive development: Research models and fugitive findings. In R. H. Wozniak & K. W. Fischer (Eds.), *Development in context: Acting and thinking in specific environments*. Lawrence Erlbaum Associates, Inc.

Bronfenbrenner, U. (2005). *Making human beings human: Bioecological perspectives on human development*. Sage Publications Ltd.

Bronfenbrenner, U., & Morris, P. A. (2006). The Bioecological Model of Human Development. In R. M. Lerner & W. Damon (Eds.), *Handbook of child psychology: Theoretical models of human development*. John Wiley & Sons, Inc..

Brunzell, T., Stokes, H., & Waters, L. (2016). Trauma-informed positive education: Using positive psychology to strengthen vulnerable students. *Contemporary School Psychology, 20*(1), 63-83.

Brunzell, T., Stokes, H., & Waters, L. (2019). Shifting teacher practice in trauma-affected classrooms: Practice pedagogy strategies within a trauma-informed positive education model. *School Mental Health, 11*(3), 600-614.

Cait, C.A. (2016). Relational theory. In N. Coady & P. Lehmann (Eds.), *Theoretical perspectives for direct social work practice: A generalist-eclectic approach*. Springer Publishing Company.

Campbell C.M. (2015). Popular Punitivism: Finding a balance between the politics, presentation, and fear of crime, *Sociology Compass, 9*(3), 180-195.

Conroy, J., & Perryman, K. (2022). Treating trauma with child-centered play therapy through the secure lens of polyvagal theory. *International Journal of Play Therapy, 31*(3), 143-152.

Covey, S.R. (2013). *The 7 habits of highly effective people: Powerful lessons in personal change*. Simon & Schuster.

Crawford, M. (2020). Ecological systems theory: Exploring the development of the theoretical framework as conceived by Bronfenbrenner. *Journal of Public Health Issues and Practices, 4*(2), 170-176.

Cruz, R.A., & Rodl, J.E. (2018). Crime and punishment: An examination of school context and student characteristics that predict out-of-school suspension. *Children and Youth Services Review, 95*, 226-234.

Deci, E.L. & Ryan, R.M. (1985). *Intrinsic motivation and self-determination in human behaviour*. Plenum.

Deci, E.L., Koestner, R., & Ryan, R.M. (1999). A meta-analytic review of experiments examining the effects of extrinsic rewards on intrinsic motivation. *Psychological Bulletin, 125*(6), 627-668.

Deci, E.L., Koestner, R., & Ryan, R.M. (2001). Extrinsic rewards and intrinsic motivation in education: Reconsidered once again. *Review of Educational Research, 71*(1), 1-27.

Department of Education Victoria. (2023, April 19). *High impact teaching strategies (HITS)*. Accessed 15 January 2024. www.education.vic.gov.au/school/teachers/teachingresources/practice/ improve/Pages/hits.aspx

Department of Education Victoria. (2023, September 4). *Victorian teaching and learning model (VTLM)*. www.education.vic.gov.au/school/teachers/teachingresources/practice/improve/Pages/Victorianteachingandlearningmodel.aspx

Department of Education, Skills and Employment Modelling (DESEM). (2022, August 8). *Teacher workforce shortages – Issues paper*. Accessed 10 January 2024. https://ministers.education.gov.au/clare/teacher-workforce-shortages-issues-paper

Dix, P. (2017). *When the adults change, everything changes: Seismic shifts in school behaviour*. Independent Thinking Press.

Downie, J., & Llewellyn, J.J. (2011). *Being relational: Reflections on relational theory and health law*. UBC Press.

Dunlap, G., Iovannone, R., Kincaid, D., Wilson, K., Christiansen, K., Strain, P.S., & Knoster, T. (2018). *Prevent-teach-reinforce: The school-based model of individualised positive behaviour support* (2nd ed.). Brookes Publishing Company.

Dweck, C.S. (2006). *Mindset: The new psychology of success*. Random House.

Egeberg, H., McConney, A., & Price, A. (2016). Classroom management and national professional standards for teachers: A review of the literature on theory and practice. *Australian Journal of Teacher Education, 41*(7), 1-18.

Erchul, W. P., & Raven, B. H. (1997). Social power in school consultation: A contemporary view of French and Raven's bases of power model. *Journal of School Psychology, 35*(2), 137-171.

Feldman, D.C., Ng, T.W.H. and Vogel, R.M. (2012). Off-the-job embeddedness: A reconceptualization and agenda for future research. In J.J. Martocchio, A. Joshi, & H. Liao (Eds.), Research in personnel and human resources management – Volume 31. Emerald Group Publishing Limited.

Foucault, M. (1977). *Discipline and punish: The birth of the prison.* Pantheon Books.

Foucault, M. (1980). *Power/knowledge: Selected interviews and other writings, 1972-79.* Pantheon.

Freire, P. (1970). *Pedagogy of the oppressed.* Seabury Press

French, J. & Raven, B. (1959). The bases of social power. In D. Cartwright (Ed.), *Studies in social power.* The University of Michigan.

Gragg, S., & Collet, V. (2023) The impact of a relationship-building strategy on teachers' perceptions of pre-schooler behaviour: A 2 x 10 approach. *Early Years, 43*(1), 182–196.

Gray, J., Kruse, S., & Tarter, C.J. (2015). Enabling school structures, collegial trust and academic emphasis. *Educational Management Administration and Leadership, 44*(6), 875–891.

Greer, D.C. (2017). Motivation and attention as foundations for student learning. In J.C. Horvath, J.M. Lodge, & J. Hattie (Eds.), *From the laboratory to the classroom: Translating science of learning for teachers.* Routledge.

Gregory, A., Skiba, R.J., & Noguera, P.A. (2010a). The achievement gap and the discipline gap: Two sides of the same coin? *Educational Researcher, 39*(1), 59–68.

Gregory, A., Cornell, D., Fan, X., Sheras, P., Shih, T.H., & Huang, F. (2010b). Authoritative school discipline: High school practices associated with lower bullying and victimization. *Journal of Educational Psychology, 102*(2), 483–496.

Gregory, A., Skiba, R.J., & Mediratta, K. (2017). Eliminating disparities in school discipline: A framework for intervention. *Review of Research in Education, 41*(1), 253–278.

Harden, B.J., Parra, L.J., & Duncan, A.D. (2019). The influence of trauma exposure on children's outcomes. In C.C. Panlilio (Ed.), *Trauma-Informed Schools: Integrating child maltreatment, prevention, detection and intervention.* Springer.

Hart, H., & Rubia, K. (2012). Neuroimaging of child abuse: A critical review. *Frontiers in Human Neuroscience,* 6, Article 52.

Hattie, J. (2008). *Visible learning.* Routledge.

Hattie, J. (2023). *Visible learning: The sequel.* Routledge.

Hayes, N., O' Toole, L., & Halpenny, A.M. (2017). *Introducing Bronfenbrenner: A guide for practitioners and students in early years education.* Routledge.

Hoffmann, F. (2016). From suspended to destitute: The disproportionate effect of out-of-school suspensions on low-income families. *Indiana Journal of Law and Social Equality, 5*(1), 169–196.

Horn, S.R., Miller-Graff, L.E., Galano, M.M., & Graham-Bermann, S.A. (2017). Posttraumatic stress disorder in children exposed to intimate partner violence: The clinical picture of physiological arousal symptoms. *Child Care in Practice, 23*(1), 90–103.

Hom, P.W., Lee, T.W., Shaw, J.D., & Hausknecht, J.P. (2017). One hundred years of employee turnover theory and research. *Journal of Applied Psychology, 102*(3), 530–545.

Jeong, Y., & Copeland, S.R. (2020). Comparing functional behaviour assessment-based interventions and non-functional behaviour assessment-based interventions: A systematic review of outcomes and methodological quality of studies. *Journal of Behaviour Education,* 29, 1–41.

Kovach, M. (2020). Leader influence: A research review of French & Raven's (1959) power dynamics. *Journal of Values-Based Leadership, 13*(2), 1–10.

Krezmien, M.P., Leone, P.E., & Achilles, G.M. (2006). Suspension, race, and disability: Analysis of statewide practices and reporting. *Journal of Emotional and Behavioral Disorders, 14*(4), 217–226.

Lampert, J., McPherson, A., & Burnett, B. (2023). Still standing: an ecological perspective on teachers remaining in hard-to-staff schools, *Teachers and Teaching*.

Lewis, R. (2008). *The developmental management approach to classroom behaviour: Responding to individual needs*. ACER Press.

Lewis, R., Romi, S., Qui, X., & Katz, Y.J. (2005). Teachers' classroom discipline and student misbehaviour in Australia, China and Israel. *Teaching and Teacher Education, 21*(6), 729–741.

Lewis, R., Romi, S., Katz, Y.J., & Qui, X. (2008). Students' reaction to classroom discipline in Australia, Israel, and China. *Teaching and Teacher Education, 24*(3), 715–724.

Martin, W. (2010). Popular Punitivism — The Role of the Courts in the Development of Criminal Justice Policies. *Australian & New Zealand Journal of Criminology, 43*(1), 1–16.

Menzies, K. (2019). Understanding the Australian Aboriginal experience of collective, historical and intergenerational trauma. *International Social Work, 62*(6), 1522–1534.

Mielke, M., & Farrington, D.P. (2021). School-based interventions to reduce suspension and arrest: A meta-analysis. *Aggression and Violent Behaviour, 56*, 101518.

Mowen, T.J., Brent, J.J., & Boman, J.H. (2020). The effect of school discipline on offending across time. *Justice Quarterly, 37*(4), 739–760. https://doi.org/10.1080/07418825.2019.1625428

National Child Traumatic Stress Network Schools Committee. (2008, October). *Child trauma toolkit for educators*. Accessed 19 January 2024. https://www.nctsn.org/sites/default/files/resources//child_trauma_toolkit_educators.pdf

National Child Traumatic Stress Network (NCTSN). (2023, September 29). *About child trauma*. Accessed 13 January 2024. https://www.nctsn.org/what-is-child-trauma/about-child-trauma

New Zealand Ministry of Education. (2014). *Restorative Practice KETE Book 2*. Accessed 19 January 2024. https://pb4l.tki.org.nz/PB4L-Restorative-Practice

Ng, T.W., & Feldman, D.C. (2014). Community embeddedness and work outcomes: The mediating role of organizational embeddedness. *Human Relations, 67*(1), 71–103.

Nicholson-Crotty, S., Birchmeier, Z., & Valentine, D. (2009). Exploring the impact of school discipline on racial disproportion in the juvenile justice system. *Social Science Quarterly, 90*(4), 1003–1018.

Organisation for Economic Co-operation and Development (OECD). (2023). *Education Policy Outlook in Australia – OECD Education Policy Perspectives* (No. 67), OECD Publishing.

Panlilio, C.C., Ferrara, A., & MacNeill, L. (2019). *Trauma, self-regulation, and learning*. In C.C. Panlilio (Ed.), *Trauma-Informed Schools: Integrating child maltreatment, prevention, detection and intervention*. Springer.

Paramita, P.P., Anderson, A., & Sharma, U. (2020). Effective teacher professional learning on classroom behaviour management: A review of literature. *Australian Journal of Teacher Education, 45*(1).

Peyton, T., Zigarmi, D., & Fowler, S.N. (2018). Examining the relationship between leaders' power use, followers' motivational outlooks, and followers' work intentions. *Frontiers in Psychology, 9*(2620), 1-20.

Porges, S. (2011). *The polyvagal theory.* Norton.

Porges, S.W. (1995). Orienting in a defensive world: Mammalian modifications of our evolutionary heritage. A Polyvagal Theory. *Psychophysiology, 32*(4), 301-318.

Pratt, T.C., Cullen, F.T., Blevins, K.R., Daigle, L.E., & Madensen, T.D. (2006). The empirical status of deterrence theory: A meta-analysis. In F. T. Cullen, J. P. Wright, & K. R. Blevins (Eds.), *Taking stock: The status of criminological theory.* Transaction Publishers

Raby, R. (2010). The intricacies of power relations in discourses of secondary school disciplinary strategies. In Z. Millei, T.G. Griffiths, & R.J. Parkes (Eds.), *Re-theorizing discipline in education: Problems, politics and possibilities.* Peter Lang.

Raby, R. (2012). *School rules: obedience, discipline and elusive democracy.* University of Toronto Press.

Raskolnikov, A. (2021). Deterrence theory: Key findings and challenges. In B. van Rooij, & D. D. Sokol (Eds.), *The Cambridge Handbook of Compliance.* Cambridge University Press.

Raven, B.H. (1965). Social influence and power. In I. Steiner & M. Fishbein (Eds.), *Current studies in social psychology.* Holt, Rinehart and Winston.

Reimer, K.E. (2019). Relationships of control and relationships of engagement: How educator intentions intersect with student experiences of restorative justice. *Journal of Peace Education, 16*(1), 49-77.

Reinke, W.M., Herman, K.C., Stormont, M., Newcomer, L., & David, K. (2013). Illustrating the multiple facets and levels of fidelity of implementation to a teacher classroom management intervention. *Adm Policy Ment Health, 40*(6), 494-506.

Rogers, B. (2007). *Behaviour management: A whole school approach.* Paul Chapman Publishing.

Rogers, B. (2015). *Classroom behaviour: A practical guide to effective teaching, behaviour management and colleague support* (4th ed.). SAGE Publications.

Roberts, P., & Green, B. (2013). Researching rural places: On social justice and rural education. *Qualitative Inquiry, 19*(10), 765-774.

Ryan, R.M., & Deci, E.L. (2017). *Self-determination Theory: Basic psychological needs in motivation, development, and wellness.* Guilford Press.

Samudre, M.D., Ackerman, K.B., & Allday, A. (2020). A systemic review of general educator training with Functional Behaviour Assessments. *Journal of Disability Policy Studies, 31*(1), 3-14.

Sinek, S. (2011). *Start with why: How great leaders inspire everyone to take action.* Penguin Books.

Skiba, R.J., Michael, R.S., Nardo, A.C., & Peterson, R.L. (2002). The color of discipline: Sources of racial and gender disproportionality in school punishment. *The Urban Review, 34*(4), 317-342.

Skiba, R.J., Arredondo, M.I., & Williams, N.T. (2014). More than a metaphor: The contribution of exclusionary discipline to a school-to-prison pipeline. *Equity & Excellence in Education, 47*(4), 546-564.

Stanley, K., & Kuo, N. (2022). 'It Takes a Village': Approaching the development of school-family-community partnerships through Bronfenbrenner's socio-ecological perspectives. *Journal of Human Sciences and Extension, 10*(1), 1-15.

Stokes, H., & Brunzell, T. (2019). Professional learning in trauma informed positive education: Moving school communities from trauma affected to trauma aware. *School Leadership Review, 14*(2).

Stokes, H., & Brunzell, T. (2020). Leading trauma-informed practice in schools. *Leading & Managing, 26*(1), 70-77. Accessed 14 January 2024. https://www.berrystreet.org.au/uploads/main/Files/Research-Articles/Stokes-Brunzell_2020_Leading-trauma-informed-schools_Leading-Managing.pdf

Stokes, H., Kern, P., Turnbull, M., Farrelly, A., & Forster, R. (2019). *Trauma informed positive education: Research and Evaluation of the Berry Street Education Model (BSEM) as a whole school approach to student engagement and wellbeing (2016-2018).* Melbourne Graduate School of Education.

Sutherland, K.S., Conroy, M.A., McLeod, B.D., Kunemund, R., & McKnight, K. (2019). Common practice elements for improving social, emotional, and behavioural outcomes of young elementary school students. *Journal of Emotional and Behavioural Disorders, 27*(2), 76-85.

Talwar, V., & Lee, K. (2011). A punitive environment fosters children's dishonesty: A natural experiment. *Child development, 82*(6), 1751-1758.

Tauber, R.T. (1986). French and Raven's power bases: A Focus for educational researchers and practitioners. *Australian Journal of Education, 30*(3), 256-265.

Teicher, M.H., Andersen, S.L., Polcari, A., Anderson, C.M., Navalta, C.P., & Kim, D.M. (2003). The neurobiological consequences of early stress and childhood maltreatment. *Neuroscience and Biobehavioral Reviews, 27*(1-2), 33-44.

Thorsborne, M., & Vinegrad, D. (2004). *Restorative practices in classrooms: Rethinking behaviour management.* Inyahead Press.

Tudge, J.R.H. (2016). Implicit versus explicit ways of using Bronfenbrenner's bioecological theory. *Human Development, 59*(4), 195-199.

Vygotsky, L.S. (1978). *Mind and society: The development of higher psychological processes.* Harvard University Press.

Waguespack, A., Vaccaro, T., & Continere, L. (2006). Functional behavioural assessment and intervention with emotional/behaviourally disordered students: In pursuit of state of the art. *International Journal of Behavioural Consultation and Therapy, 2*(4), 463-474.

Wlodkowski, R.J. (1983). *Motivational opportunities for successful teaching* (Leader's Guide). Universal Dimensions.

www.ingramcontent.com/pod-product-compliance
Lightning Source LLC
Chambersburg PA
CBHW071912110526
44591CB00011B/1656